Wigmaking

step
by
step

Part 1
Weft work

Jean Anderson

JA Publications

ISBN 0 9519080 0 6

First published 1992

JA Publications
12a Upper Old Street
Stubbington
Fareham
Hampshire
PO14 3LJ

Printed in Great Britain by Dotesios Ltd, Trowbridge, Wiltshire

Contents

Contents

Foreword

It is a pleasure to be asked to write a foreword to this book on Wigmaking - the first, to my knowledge, since Botham and Sharrad.

Wigmaking is a craft which, in many ways preceded Hairdressing (although they have been very close) by the fact that the Hairdresser dressed the postiche from the Wigmaker. This, however, should not stop anyone from considering a career in Wigmaking and Postiche.

It is with this in mind that I hope the book will attract many people to consider the various aspects of this craft...

...for the Hairdresser, to extend their knowledge and skills (for example, Christopher Dove, who is an excellent Hairdresser and makes all his postiche for his Hairdressing shows)...

...for the Make-up Artist, who wishes to specialise in Stage, Film and TV work, where the camera can reveal every line in close-up...

...and for people of all walks of life - the able-bodied to the handicapped, who would like to specialise in one of the many facets of Wigmaking and Postiche - in many cases, when trained, working from their own homes.

The book follows all areas of work undertaken in the making of Wigs and Postiche in a clear and easy-to-follow method - this, coupled with a practical application, to enable the student to build up speed and understanding (which is required by industry) of the whole process. In this day of *machine versus person*, many skills have been lost. I hope this book will inspire people to keep one area of *hand-made* alive and flourishing, to the benefit of all who wear and use Postiche and Wigs.

John A Walton *Chief Southern Regional Assessor for Hairdressing and Wigmaking, SRCET*

Preparation of cuttings and combings

You will learn the differences between cuttings and combings, the way they are prepared for use in wigmaking and why it is necessary to carry out these processes. You should also develop a 'feel' for hair.

To prepare for this section

Gather together as much hair as you can from brushes and combs.

Save some hair that has been cut from a client's head.

Tools required

Hackle

Clamps

String

Drawing brushes

Pair of scissors or blunt blade of a knife

Two bowls

Towels

Pocket comb

How much do you know about the hair itself?

See if you can complete the diagram by filling in the blanks.

The outer layer of the hair, the

....

is made up of

....

scales which point

....

These are similar to

....

The next layer (working inwards)
is called the

....

and contains the

....

pigment of the hair.

Also found in this layer are the

....

which are affected when
permanently curling the hair.

The middle or core of the hair is
called the

....

This has

....

spaces which reflect the light,
causing hair to shine.

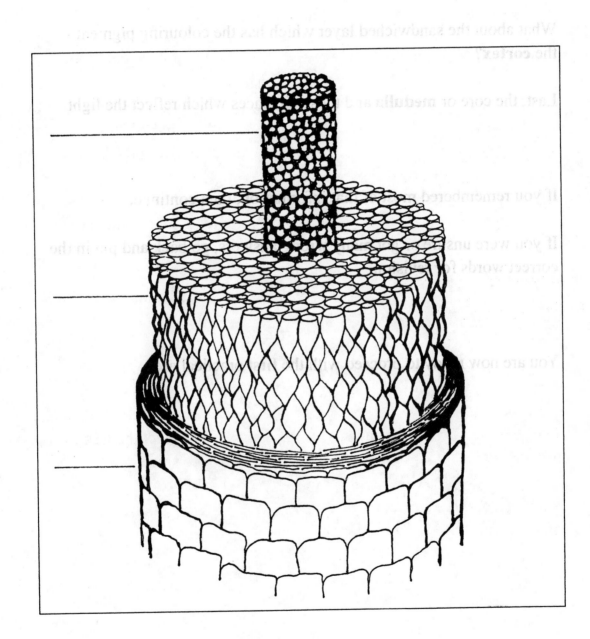

How well did you do?

Did you remember the outer layer as the **cuticle**, with overlapping scales pointing away from the scalp?

What about the sandwiched layer which has the colouring pigment - the **cortex**?

Last, the core or **medulla** and those airspaces which reflect the light.

If you remembered most of that information, then continue.

If you were unsure or got many wrong answers, go back and put in the correct words for revision.

You are now ready to proceed with the first practical area.

Preparation of combings

Take the hair that you have collected from brushes and combs.
Remove a single hair from the pile.
Can you see the hair bulb - a small, white blob at one end?

Run your fingers from the bulb, first one way, then the other.
Notice how it feels rough one way, yet smooth the other.
What do you think is causing this sensation?

If your answer was the scales of the cuticle layer, then you were correct.

The hair bulb is the root of the hair.
Therefore, your pile of hair has all its roots and points mixed up.

What do you think would happen if we worked with hair in this state?

Yes, it would tangle.

We have all heard of the 'shredded wheat' effect!

Look carefully at your bundle of **combings**.

Combings are the natural hairfall found in brushes and combs.

Can you imagine how long it would take, if we had to sort out each individual hair by looking for the bulb, then placing all the bulbs together?

I am going to show you the easy way.

Sorting out the roots from the points takes seven stages.

Stage one

Take a small handful of combings.
Gently pull them apart and shake.
Notice how dust and dirt, as well
as tiny pieces of hair, fall from
your hands.
Continue doing this until the hair is
reasonably loose.

This process is called **loosening** or
teasing.

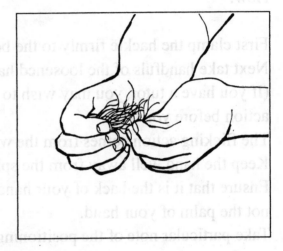

Stage two

Hackling

A hackle is a piece of wood with a series of metal prongs set obliquely.
These spikes are very sharp and the hackle must be clamped to the bench
during use.
Also, it is essential to keep the spikes covered when not in use.

So, how do we use it and what does it do?

The hackle frees the hair you have collected from knots.
It disentangles the hair.

How?

First clamp the hackle firmly to the bench.
Next take handfuls of the loosened hair and flick it through the hackle.
(If you have a tutor, you may wish to ask for a demonstration of this action before you try.)
The flicking action comes from the wrist not the elbow.
Keep the hand well away from the spikes.
Ensure that it is the back of your hand which moves towards the hackle not the palm of your hand.
Take particular note of the positioning of the hand in the diagram.

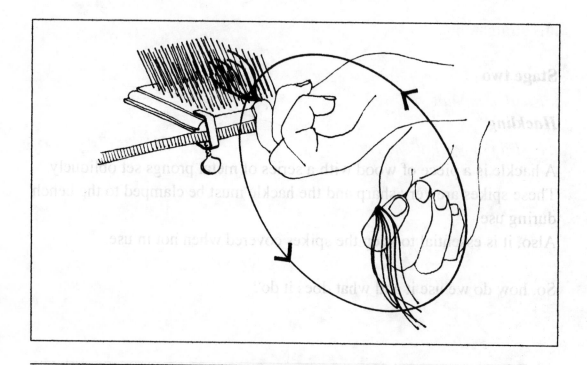

When one side of the hair is free from its tangles, turn it around and hackle the other side.
Keep taking handfuls of the hair and hackling until all the hair is free from tangles.
The hair is now straightened.

Clean the hackle (draw a comb across the hackle, between the spikes to remove any remaining hair), cover and put away.

How did you get on?

Did you need any plasters?

What can we now say about the hair?

It is straight, but...

it still has all its roots and points mixed up,
it is still a mixture of lengths
and
it is still not level at one end.

Stage three

Place the straightened hair into the drawing brushes or carding mats.
Using the blade of a pair of scissors or the blunt edge of a knife and the thumb, gently draw off a few strands of hair (about three or four).
Place them level into your left hand.
Do not take too much hair at a time.

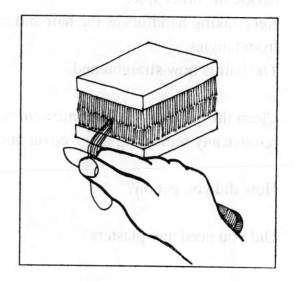

Once you feel you have as much in your left hand as you can handle, place the level end to the edge of the bench.

Continue in this way until all the hair has been **drawn off level**.

The hair is now straight and level at one end, but the

....
and the

....
are still mixed up and there are many different

....

Stage four

Stage four sorts out the hair into its different lengths -
a process called **drawing off in lengths.**

Place the level end of the hair into the drawing brushes.
As before, you are going to draw off the hair, using the thumb and a
blade, only this time you are going to draw off the longest hair only.

Once done, tie about 5cms from the now level end.

Place onto the bench.

Next draw off the second longest hair and tie 5cms from the now
level end.

Place onto the bench.

Carry on drawing off each length until all the hair over 8cms in length is
tied up into bundles.
Any hair which is shorter than 8cms can be thrown away.

The hair is now straightened, in its
different lengths and has a
level end.
All that remains is for us to sort out
the roots from the points.

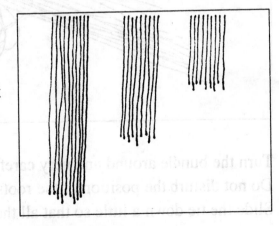

Stage five

Turning

Step one
Take a bowl of warm soapy water and a bowl of warm clear water.
You will also need a towel.

Take each section of hair in turn and holding by the tie, vigorously swish
the longer end in the soapy water.
This will cause the points to run back whilst the roots will stay forward.

You can emphasise this by gently rubbing back and forth with the finger
whilst the bundle is held against the side of the bowl.

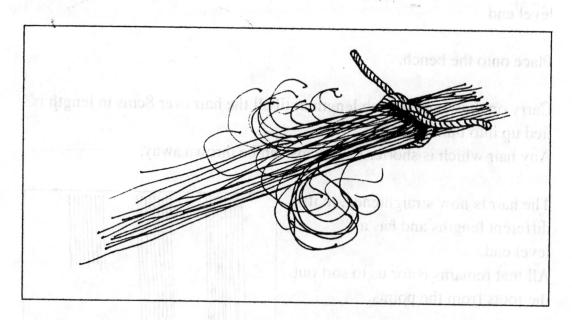

Turn the bundle around and very carefully, wash the other end.
Do not disturb the position of the roots and points.
Slide the tie down a little so that all the hair has been cleaned.

Now, extremely carefully, rinse the hair in the bowl of clear water. It is important that the positions of the roots and points are not disturbed.

Place the bundle onto a towel and very gently, squeeze out the excess moisture - again the

.... must not be allowed to move. Treat each bundle in this way.

Allow the bundles to dry naturally. 24 hours is usually enough time. If time is at a premium, then a postiche oven may be used.

Now spend 15 minutes answering the following.

1 *What would happen if we did not sort out the roots from the points?*
2 *Which process is used to allow the dust and debris to fall?*
3 *What care must be taken when hackling and why?*
4 *What is meant by 'drawing off'?*
5 *Name the two different methods of drawing off used so far.*
6 *What is the shortest length of hair that is of use in wigmaking?*
7 *What happens to the roots and points during turning?*
8 *What equipment have you used so far for turning?*

How did you get on?

Did you have to refer back?

Stage six

Turning

Step two
Look at the bundles of hair.
You should be able to distinguish between the roots and the points.
Remember, the points have run back but the roots have stayed forward.
All that remains now is for you to put the roots together.

Fix the hackle to the bench.

What precautions should you take?

....

....

Work with each bundle in turn.
Cut the tie and remove the string.
Place into the hackle, allowing the roots to protrude at the front and the
points to be behind the second row of spikes.
Put a pocket comb between the first and second rows of spikes.
That is between the

.... and the

.... of the hair.

14

Draw off the roots as you have drawn off before.
The roots must be placed level in the left hand.
Turn the remaining hair around (roots are now facing you) and draw off.
Place the level end to the edge of the bench.

What are you left with?

Hair with the

.... towards the edge of the bench

and the

.... away from the edge of the bench.

Tie each length 5cms from the root end.
This is the level end.
Carry out this procedure with each bundle.

This means that you have finally sorted out the roots from the points.

Stage seven

This is only needed if the hair is not perfectly level at the root end.
Place the hair into the drawing brushes so that the roots are protruding.
Draw off level.

When you have a manageable amount, tie about 5cms from the roots.
Continue until all the hair has been drawn off level and is tied.

Congratulations!
You have succeeded in preparing your bundle of combings ready for use
in wigmaking.
Store until required. The container must be labelled and mothproof.

Preparation of cuttings

When cutting hair that is of a good length and may be useful in the
wigmaking room, follow these rules where possible.

Try to keep all the roots together.
If this is achieved, then all that is needed is for the hair to be drawn off
level.

Keep all the different lengths together.
If this has not been possible then the hair must be treated as for
combings.

All hair should be checked for infestation.
If there are any 'nits' adhering to the hair, then the hair must be cleansed
and sterilised.
Also for 'nits' there is a 'nitting machine'. This apparatus fits in front of
the hackle.
As the hair is drawn through the hackle, the 'nits' fall into a waiting tray
and are subsequently burned.

Sources and varieties of hair

In this section, I will explain where hair comes from and the advantages and disadvantages of each.

Where does hair come from?

Hair collectors buy hair from persons wishing to sell their hair. These can be representatives from convents or, more usually, persons wishing to sell hair so that they can buy food. In some countries it has been known for a mother to allow her daughter to grow her hair only to sell it for money to buy food.

European hair

The best quality hair.
Poland produces brown to blonde hair.
Yugoslavia has brown colours which have red tendencies. This is also poor in quality.
Italy gives us black, dark brown, 'grey' or white hair.
Italian hair is usually sorted by hand. This is termed epilee.
White hair is the most expensive of all as the truer the dark hair of an individual, the truer the white they will become.
White hair is often bleached up from one of the above sources.
European hair is used for all types of postiche, whether they be for everyday wear, or fashion, or for cosmetic reasons.
European hair is the type most used for medical postiche.
It is also used for the better television and theatrical postiche.
Most European postiche is hand-made.

Asiatic hair

Comes from China or India. Always dark in colour.

Chinese hair is very straight and coarse.

Indian hair has warmer influences. It can have wave or curl which is usually non existent in Chinese hair.

It is also finer than Chinese hair, meaning that it can be wavy.

This type of hair can be used for all forms of postiche.

In order to gain the correct colour the hair is often bleached and then tinted to achieve the required shade. This means it fades very quickly.

Animal fibres

Yak

The coarse belly hair of the Yak (Tibetan ox) gives a black, grey/off-white hair which is used for facial postiche. It can be mixed with European hair for texture.

Mohair

This is the off-white hair from the Angora goat.

It is very soft and therefore used for competition work only.

Mohair is very expensive as it is difficult to obtain.

Horse hair

This type of hair is used for legal postiche as it is very coarse.

It is available in black or white (or a mixture to produce grey).

Synthetic fibres

These are man-made. They are flame resistant, but they will melt.
Producing a permanent curl can be made by using steam alone.

NB The hair must be on rollers at the time of steaming.

Newer, artificial products are non-static. They have a more natural feel to
them, due to a simulated cuticle.
These fibres can reflect light. All colours are available.

Whereas human hair can be used for all postiche, the use of synthetic
fibres is limited.

Wigs made of synthetic fibres

Where these are hand made, it is usual for the hair to be tied onto a
flexible base.

Commercially, these pieces are made to a set pattern - a blueprint. The
'wig houses' produce a prototype which they test out. If this produces
satisfactory results, then fibres are hackled, cut, bleached and
transformed into the correct colour and length required. These are then
stitched by machine to form a weft.

Two methods

1 *Stitch across hair then fold in half and restitch.*
2 *Fold the hair over a length of fine string and stitch once only.*

These fibres can then be curled by being subjected to controlled temperatures, whilst being rolled onto aluminium curlers.

It is important to allow the weft to cool after heating.

A lace frame is produced.
Onto this is stitched, lightly, a plastic foundation.
This has the design for the style imprinted onto it.

Stitch the weft as the pattern states.

Remove the plastic foundation.

If the front is to be hand knotted or implanted, then this is done at this point.

Make and stitch into position, the required tension elastics.

So let us list the main advantages and disadvantages of the different types of hair.

Hair	Advantage	Disadvantage
Asian hair	Inexpensive	Coarse texture Small colour range Chemically treated Condition unreliable Unusual to have curl
European hair	Available through NHS Hand made Comfortable Natural-looking Good fit Many colours available Fine texture	Hair expensive Requires professional operators Needs skilled care

Animal fibres	Advantage	Disadvantage
Mohair	Takes any colour well, therefore is ideal for competition work	Due to its soft characteristics, it is liable to tangle with frequent use
Yak	Cheap Can be dyed to almost any shade	Restricted colours
Horse hair	Used for legal postiche only	Not suitable for normal wearing

Synthetic fibres	Advantage	Disadvantage
	Cheaper NHS available Easy to clean Labour inexpensive Limited skill needed Off-the-shelf availability Good colour range	Can make the wearer uncomfortably hot

Various factors have been mentioned regarding the choice of hair or artificial hair for postiche.

The major considerations are as follows:

Client comfort

The availability of the desired hair

The cost of the hair

Whether the client requires a hand made piece

Whether the client requires a made to measure piece

The intended use of the postiche

The ease to the client of maintaining the postiche

Disinfection and disinfestation of hair

In this section, I shall explain how we clean hair which might be contaminated.

The equipment and materials used are detailed in the passage.

Disinfection is the way we destroy or prevent the growth of bacteria.

Disinfestation is the way we destroy and remove such infestations as the pediculosis capitis, the head louse (nit) and its eggs.

Why is it necessary for you to know how to remove any infestation or infection?

It is possible that hair supplied may be infected or infested.
Where could this have come from?

Hair may have been cut from an infested head. Hair is often purchased in other countries and then shipped in the hold to this country. Many different forms of 'life' may be present in the hold of a ship. It has been known for the spore Tuberculous baccillis, the TB spore, to be present on hair.

A client may supply the hair him/herself. Perhaps it was cut as a child. This hair may be infected or infested without the knowledge of the client. **It is therefore very important that any spores etc are removed, both for the health of the wigmaker and for the intended wearer.**

To remove infection it is usual to employ a chemical treatment of some kind.

To remove infestation we use chemical treatments and a 'nitting' machine or very fine toothed comb.

It is important that a **boardworker** (a person who makes postiche of any kind) does not use any chemical or other means to kill bacteria or infestation which might impair the colour or elasticity of the hair.

Equipment used during these processes

Bowl	This must be able to withstand the chemicals it is intended to hold. It is used for both chemicals and water so it is important to rinse the bowl thoroughly after each use.
Gloves	Used to protect the skin from the chemicals that are used. Gloves must be washed and dusted with talcum powder after each use.
'Nitting' machine	This machine is used to remove dead lice and 'nits'. Immediately following use, the machine requires cleaning and disinfecting. The 'nitting' machine must be stored very carefully.
Hackle	The hackle is used in conjunction with the 'nitting' machine, which is attached in front of the hackle during use. The hackle must be

clamped to the bench during use. After use, it requires cleaning and disinfecting, then storing carefully. The hackle must be covered when not in use.

Fine toothed comb Also used to remove dead lice and 'nits'. Clean and disinfect thoroughly after use.

Postiche oven A very low-temperature oven used when drying postiche. Regular checks on the safety of the wiring and the plug tops is needed. Switch off after use.

Towels Used to blot the hair during cleansing. All towels must be washed after use.

Storage container The container should be clean and clearly labelled. It is also important for the container to be mothproof.

Materials used during these processes

Chemical
disinfectants

Used to destroy bacteria. Always read the manufacturer's instructions before commencing the process. Then follow them exactly. Label, in a clear way, all bottles containing chemicals. All chemicals should be handled and stored carefully. Avoid contact with the skin.

Disinfestants

Liquids which are used to kill lice and 'nits'. Always read the manufacturer's instructions before commencing the process. Then follow them exactly. Bottles containing chemicals must be clearly labelled. All chemicals should be handled and stored with caution. Avoid contact with the skin.

Conditioner

After the hair has been subjected to these chemicals, it is advisable to comb conditioner through, then rinse, to condition dry hair.

Disinfecting hair

Hair arrives in this country in hanks or plaits.

First cut the tie and remove the string.
Tie the hair back together in smaller bundles, leaving the tie loose
enough to slide up the bundle slightly during washing.

Next, taking great care not to tangle the hair, wash the hair to remove
any grease or debris that may be present.

Where disinfectant is needed, use a proprietary brand.
Read and follow the manufacturer's instructions.

After disinfection has been completed, rinse the hair carefully.

Follow this by conditioning it to smooth the cuticle layer.

Blot the hair on a towel, then dry in a postiche oven.

The hair should then be placed into a clearly labelled mothproof
container and stored until required.

Disinfesting hair

If the hair which has been supplied to you was infested, you would need to remove the infestation first.

Most products made for this purpose contain **malathion** or **carbaryl**.
Read the manufacturer's instructions before you begin.
These instructions must be followed.

Rinse and dry the hair before disinfesting.

If it is necessary to use the 'nitting' machine, secure it firmly to the bench in front of the hackle.
The hair is then drawn through the hackle and the 'nitting' machine together.
This removes both the lice and the 'nits', allowing them to drop from the hair into a tray.
The contents of the tray are then burned.

If a 'nitting' machine is not available, then a fine toothed comb can be used as an alternative.
Holding the hair over a piece of tissue paper, draw the comb through the hair, allowing the infestation to drop.
Dispose of the 'nits' and lice safely.

Rinse and condition as needed, then dry the hair.

Tie at the roots and store in a mothproof, clearly labelled container.

Disinfection and disinfestation revision test

Without referring back to the text or your notes, answer the following on a separate sheet:

1 What is the difference between disinfection and disinfestation?

2 Name two ways in which hair can become contaminated.

3 What is the main reason for removing the contamination?

4 What is a Boardworker?

5 Why are gloves used?

6 Why is a 'nitting' machine used?

7 Where is a 'nitting' machine fixed?

8 Why is it necessary to cover a hackle when it is not being used?

9 If a 'nitting' machine is not available, what other piece of equipment can be used?

10 What checks are needed for the postiche oven?

11 The container used for storing hair must be -?- and -?-

12 For what purpose is a chemical disinfectant used?

13 For what purpose is a chemical disinfestant used?

14 *What is the first thing you must carry out when using a proprietary brand of chemical?*

15 *Name three precautions to take when handling chemicals*

16 *What is the reason for using a conditioner after one of these processes?*

17 *How does hair usually arrive in this country?*

18 *How are dust and debris removed?*

19 *What is usually contained in proprietary chemicals used for disinfesting? (-?- or -?-)*

20 *How are lice and 'nits' disposed of?*

How do you feel you answered the questions?
If you are satisfied that you know most of the facts, then proceed to the next lesson.
If you are unsure, re-do the test using the text and your notes.

Mixing and matching hair

Prior to this lesson, look at the various heads around you as you go about your daily tasks. Mentally note what you see.

Think back to the heads that you have observed. What did you notice?

Write down three points that you saw.

....

....

....

Have you identified that there are many different colours, textures and lengths of hair?

Let us look a bit further into these and other factors involved in hair.

Different colours

No head of hair is made up of a single colour.
The visual appearance is made up from a combination of shades.
For example hair may have red tones, gold tones and ashen tones.
Hair also may have a percentage of white hair present.
Please note that there is no such thing as 'grey' hair - it is white hair
mixed in with the wearer's own colour. In fact there could be any
combination of these tones and white.

It is not possible for a wigmaker to have in stock, every colour that may
be required. Therefore, the wigmaker has to know how to mix and match
hair to the necessary shade.

Different textures

When making postiche to match a client's own hair, an exact match is
needed if the piece is to be disguised effectively.
This means that, not only have we to consider the colour, but also the
texture of the client's hair.

Imagine a little old lady with very fine hair. She has had an accident
which has caused her to lose most of the hair on her crown. This is
causing her a lot of distress, so her doctor has recommended a National
Health Service hairpiece to help her. Just think of the disastrous effect a
piece of postiche made from very thick coarse hair could give.

A wigmaker has to be aware of the needs of the client. There are
therapeutic values to be considered.

Different lengths

By mixing together different lengths of hair, the wigmaker can produce a tapered effect.

Different qualities

Hair is bought from all over the world.
The best quality hair is hair in a virgin state.

What is meant by hair in a virgin state?

....

....

Did you know that it means hair that has not been treated by any chemicals?
The best quality dark hair comes from Spain and Northern Italy (in particular Tuscany).
The best brown or auburn hair comes from France.
Of course the best blonde hair is obtained from Germany.
Naturally white hair is very rare.
The darker the hair to begin with, the truer white it will turn with age.
Once again it is important that an exact match is achieved wherever possible. If the exact match is not available, then the wigmaker must make the match as close as possible.

Bearing in mind the fact that a wigmaker may never actually meet the client, spend a few moments noting how you would assume the wigmaker knows what is needed.

....

....

....

In the postiche room, or at a client's home a record card has to be made out. It is from this record card that a wigroom order form is made out. The record card should contain everything that the wigmaker might require.

Equipment used during mixing and matching

Drawing brushes   These are used to hold the hair before mixing. They must be kept free from hair and clean at all times.
They resemble two square hairbrushes, one placed upside down on the other.

Carding mats   These are another type of drawing brush. They differ in that they are leather or hardboard with metal pins pushed through.
Their use is as for drawing brushes.

Hackle	The hackle is used in the blending of the colours. It must be secured to the bench. It must be kept clean and free from hair. If a slanting hackle is used, it is essential that the pins point away from the operator. Store with a cover over the pins. It is best stored at a low level to prevent accidents when reaching for it.
Paper	The mixed hair is placed onto the paper.
Thread	Strong thread is needed for tying up the blended hair.
Record card	To be kept in a filing system so that it is there when it is required.
Workroom sample	A mesh of hair taken from the client. Used to ensure an exact match is obtained. The sample should be kept safe with the order form. It should be handled with great care.
Storage container	The container for hair must be clean, mothproof and clearly labelled.

Method

Read the workroom order.

Make notes of the colours required and their proportions to each other.

Identify the texture and length of the hair.

Check for the required quality.

Establish whether the hair has to be curled or not and to what degree.

Take the hair to be mixed.

Place each bundle into its own pair of drawing brushes.

The hair in the drawing brushes should have the roots protruding.

Fix the hackle firmly to the bench.

Place a piece of paper onto the bench. This is used for checking the match against the hair sample.

Place the predominant (main) shade into the hackle.

Allow the roots to protrude for approximately 7cms.

Slowly add some of the toning hair to the predominant shade. (If a slight overlap is allowed it makes removal easier should you put too much in.

Please note that removing hair that has been added wrongly is a very tricky procedure - one that is best avoided.)

Draw the hair through the hackle. Then, using the fingers of the right hand, knead the two colours/ textures together. Refer to the diagram.

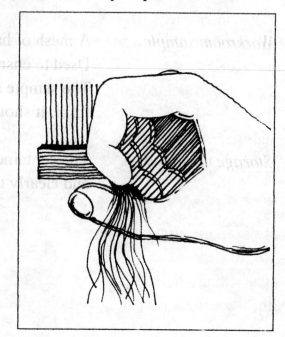

Continue hackling and kneading until the hair is an exact match.

If necessary, draw off level.

Tie at the root end and store in a labelled, mothproof container.

Faults that can happen when mixing hair and how to correct them

There are two main faults which might occur when mixing hair.
Can you think what they might be?

....

....

If you thought that an incorrect mix was one then you were correct.

The other main fault is achieving an uneven blend.

To counteract an incorrect mix

Constantly check the blend you are obtaining.
Do not take for granted that the amounts of hair you have decided upon
are correct.
This is particularly important when making percentage white hair.
The easiest way to ensure that an incorrect mix is not made is to add the
hair in small amounts.

To stop an uneven blend

The sample must be checked continuously, both against the sample from
the client and visually, in as near daylight as possible. Rhythmic hackling
and kneading help us to make sure the blend is even.

How much to mix

If 400 grams of 50% white hair is needed, we would need 200 grams of white hair and 200 grams of the main shade.
If 400 grams of 75% white hair is needed, we would need 300 grams of white hair and 100 grams of the original colour.

Following the above table you should be able to work out any amounts that might be needed.

Estimating tones is more difficult. It is usually only carried out by an experienced wigmaker. One who has an 'eye' for colour. The method used is to add the required tone, a little at a time. The hair being mixed is checked frequently against the sample from the client.

Mixing and matching revision test

Without referring back to the text or your notes, answer the following on a separate sheet:

1 *Is any head of hair made up from one single colour?*

2 *Explain how the visual colour of hair is made up?*

3 *What is meant by tones within the hair?*

4 *Explain 'grey' hair.*

5 *Would you think it likely that an experienced wigmaker would have hair of every colour in stock?*

6 *If a wigmaker required one hundred grams of 25% white hair, what amounts of hair would be required?*

7 *For what other reasons might hair need mixing?*

8 *What is meant by virgin hair?*

9 *Fill in the following table:*

The best dark hair comes from -?-

The best brown hair comes from -?-

The best -?- hair comes from Germany

The best -?- hair comes from France

The truest white hair comes from -?-

10 *Give three items that should be on a record card.*

11 *What is meant by a workroom sample?*

12 *What are the two main movements used when mixing hair?*

13 *Briefly explain how each of the two movements is carried out.*

14 *How is the hair added?*

15 *What is meant by the predominant shade?*

16 *What are the two main faults that are likely to occur?*

17 *Explain a method of counteracting one of the faults.*

Did you find that easy?

If there were many blank spaces in your answers then go back and re-do the test using the notes.

Lesson five

Permanently curling hair for use in wigmaking

In this lesson we are going to look at the reasons why hair is made curly before it is made up into postiche.

Tools and materials required

Drawing brushes

Hair

Jigger

Fine string

End tissues

Water spray

Postiche oven or drying cabinet

Bigoudi

Pan of water

You have already learned some of the necessary work that may have to be done prior to producing postiche.
Let's see how much you can remember.

After a client has decided to have a piece of postiche made a record card is made out.

Onto this card are written all the details required by the wigmaker when making the postiche - details such as:

the colour required,
the degree of curl
and
the length.

A sample of the client's own hair is advisable, particularly when matching men's postiche.

This card contains all the requirements of the client.

Another detail entered on the record card is the amount of curl required.
If the hair is to be curly, the degree of curl is recorded.
This tells the wigmaker whether a process called **frisure forcee** needs to be carried out before the postiche can be made.

Frisure forcee is the name given to the process of permanently curling hair for use in wigmaking.
Why does this process need to be carried out before the hair is made up?
Why cannot we just 'perm' it as we would a normal head of hair?

One of the reasons we have already talked about, in lesson three, disinfection and disinfestation.

Can you remember what effect these processes can have on the hair?

....

....

If you cannot remember re-read the part of lesson three that refers to conditioning. I hope you recalled that the chemicals used are likely to impair the structure of the hair.
The solutions used for 'perming' are also very strong.

A second reason and probably, a reason of far greater importance, is that the foundation is likely to become damaged. The hair can knot. This is because it is not as pliable as when it was being fed from the sebaceous glands.

The sebaceous glands produce

....

which protects and

....

the hair.

Therefore frisure forcee is the method of precurling hair for use in postiche work

Equipment used during this process

Bigoudis	These are wooden curlers of diameters to cater for the sizes of curls that may be required. They must not be affected by heat. Keep clean.

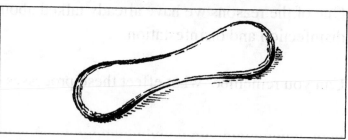

Comb	This assists when winding the curl.
Pan of boiling water	Used to make the curl permanent.
Drawing brushes	Must be kept clean and free from hair. Used for holding the hair.
Drying cabinet	Used for drying the curls. Preheat before use. Always switch off after use.
Jigger	Used to hold the hair whilst winding. See later notes.
End tissues	To hold the points of the hair neatly.
Towels	Used to blot the hair.
Scissors and thread	Used when tying the hair into bundles.
Water spray/jug	Used to hold the water.

Jigger

A rectangular piece of wood with two holes bored at one end.
There is a groove between the two holes.

A long piece of string is threaded through the two holes and tied to form
a loop.

When the jigger is clamped to the bench, this loop should hang about
5-10cms from the floor.

When the hair is placed under the string, the foot is placed onto the loop
and pressed downwards.
The hair is then held as though it is in a vice.

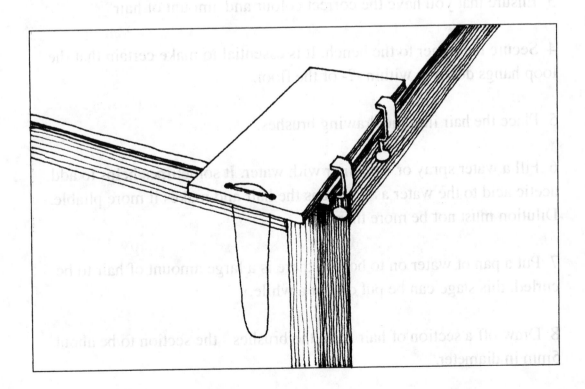

Frisure forcee

You have to produce a sample of permanently curled hair.

Method

1 Prepare your equipment as listed at the beginning of the lesson.

2 Check the record card for details of the amount of curl required for the finished postiche.

3 Ensure that you have the correct colour and amount of hair.

4 Secure the jigger to the bench. It is essential to make certain that the loop hangs down to within -?- of the floor.

5 Place the hair into the drawing brushes.

6 Fill a water spray or container with water. It sometimes helps to add acetic acid to the water as it softens the hair and makes it more pliable. Dilution must not be more than 6%.

7 Put a pan of water on to boil. If there is a large amount of hair to be curled, this stage can be put off for a while.

8 Draw off a section of hair from the brushes - the section to be about 5mm in diameter.

9 After checking up with the record card, choose a bigoudi of the correct diameter.

10 Dampen hair with water and -?- Solution no more than -?-

11 Tie the section of hair with thread at a point about 2cm from the root end. Leave ends of thread about 15cm long.

12 Place the tied end under the string on the jigger.
Place your foot into the string that is hanging under the jigger.
The hair is now being held as though it were in a vice.
It is firmly clamped.

13 Place an end tissue/paper around the points.

14 Ensuring that you maintain an even tension, wind the hair round the bigoudi as far as the tie.

15 Carefully slacken the grip you have on the hair by releasing pressure on the jigger.
Take another end paper and wrap it around the hair and the bigoudi.

16 Using the long ends of thread that were left at the beginning, tie to secure the hair into position around the bigoudi.

17 Place on one side.

18 Repeat the above until all the hair to be curled has been wound onto bigoudis.

19 The wound bigoudis are now placed very carefully into the pan of boiling water for 30 minutes.

20 After the 30 minutes have passed, the hair is then removed from the water. Again, extreme caution must be exercised.

21 Blot the bigoudis onto the towel to remove excess moisture.

22 Next, the bigoudis are placed into the postiche oven/drying cabinet until thoroughly dry.

23 Remove the papers and cut the thread. The hair is then removed from the bigoudi.

24 Place all the hair together, making sure that you keep the roots at the same end and tie about 5cms from the roots.

25 The hair is then placed into a mothproof container until required. Label the container with all the details.

Two main faults and how to avoid them

1 An uneven curl along the length of the hair.

The tension must be *firm* during winding.
The tension must be *even* during winding.
Make sure that the threads are tied securely.

2 The end result is too loose or too tight.

Make sure that you assess correctly, the diameter of bigoudi you require
for the result requested.
Do not take too much hair in the sections.

Revision test on permanently curling hair for use in wigmaking

Try to answer the following without looking back to your notes or to the text.

1 *What is the name given to the process of permanently curling hair?*

2 *Give one reason why it is necessary for the hair to be curled prior to making into postiche.*

3 *What produces sebum and what does it do?*

4 *What are bigoudis?*

5 *For what reason do we use a pan of water?*

6 *For what reason is a postiche oven used?*

7 *Why is a jigger used?*

8 *What is a jigger?*

9 *How far from the floor should the string be?*

10 *How do we make the jigger hold the hair?*

11 *Describe how the hair is held.*

12 *How does the diameter of the bigoudi affect the degree of curl?*

13 *What can be added to the water in the water spray?*

14 *What is the maximum solution that can be used?*

15 *Why is this additive used?*

16 *How many end papers are used for each bigoudi and where are they placed?*

17 *Why do we leave long ends of thread?*

18 *Briefly desribe the winding process.*

20 *How long are the bigoudis in the boiling water?*

21 *After boiling, what happens?*

22 *What type of container is used to store the hair?*

23 *How would you avoid an uneven curl along the length of the hair?*

24 *What result would be gained if the wrong diameter of bigoudi were used?*

If you answered the majority of the questions - well done.
If many were a little difficult, then repeat the exercise.

Mount the sample of permanently curled hair into your folder.

Permanently curling hair

The following methods of permanently curling hair for use in wigmaking are seldom used today.

As I have already stated, most hair which requires curling, before it is made into postiche, is curled using Frisure Forcee.

To wind the hair around a bigoudi, there must be at least 15cms length. Knowing, as you do, that hair of 8cms and over can be used in wigmaking, we need to be able to curl shorter hair.

A method called Crop Curl is used on shorter hair.

Equipment required

Drawing brushes	*Cylindrical object*
Hair to be curled	*Wire mesh tray*
Water spray	*Clip or weight*
Water, may have acetic acid added	*Pan of water*
Jigger	*Postiche oven*

The crop curl

Crop curling produces curl on hair from 8-14cms in length.

Method

1 Prepare all your equipment.

2 Place the hair to be curled into the drawing brushes.

3 Draw off a fine mesh of hair. The finer the section, the tighter the curl you will be able to produce.

4 Moisten the root end.

5 'Felt' these together by rubbing against the palm of your hand, using your thumb. This removes the need for tying each section.

6 Moisten the whole section. The water used for this, may have a few drops of acetic acid added, to make the hair more pliable.

7 The hair is then wound around a cylindrical object, for example a curler or a pencil. The diameter of the object determines the diameter of curl.
It is important to remember that the object must be smooth to allow the curl to slide off. It makes the winding far easier if the section of hair is held in the jigger, whilst winding.

8 Slide the wound hair off. It should now resemble a pincurl.

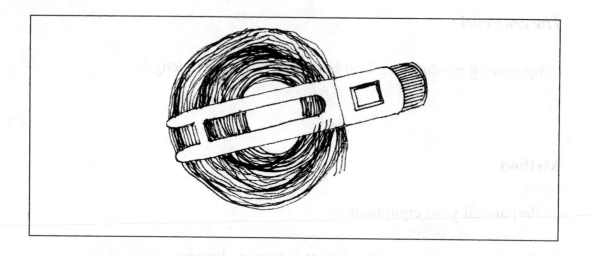

9 Place it onto a wire tray, using either a small weight or a pin clip, to keep its shape.

10 Processes 3 to 8 should be repeated until either all the hair to be curled has been wound, or a tray has been filled.

11 Place a pan, half filled with water, on to boil.

12 When the water is boiling, the wire tray full of curls is placed over it.

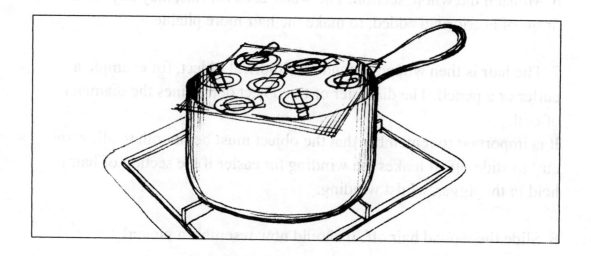

14 After the curls have been steamed, they should be allowed to cool.

15 The curls are next placed into a warm postiche oven to bake - usually for 30 minutes to one hour.

16 Remove the curls from the oven.

17 Allow to cool.

18 Tie into small bundles of short, curled hair. Remember to tie at the root end.

19 Store in a mothproof container, until required.

Long hair (usually in switches), for use in wigmaking, can be given a permanent crimp, using a method called **Creoling**.

Creoling

Hair which has been treated in this way, is most often used to give bulk to a piece of postiche.

Equipment required

Drawing brushes	*Jigger*	*Water*
Hair to be crimped	*Pan of water*	*and*
Water spray	*Postiche oven*	*dilute acetic acid*

Method

1 Prepare all equipment.

2 Place hair to be curled into the drawing brushes.

3 Draw off a section of hair. The finer the section, the tighter the crimp.

4 Moisten the root ends.

5 'Felt,' by rubbing the roots against your palm, using your thumb. Alternatively, tie the roots together.

6 Place the 'felted' or tied end under the string of the jigger.

7 Moisten the whole section. This water may have a few drops of acetic acid added to make it more pliable.

8 Plait the hair, by splitting the section into 3 even meshes and bringing each mesh from side to centre. Ensure that you use the same amount of tension with each movement.

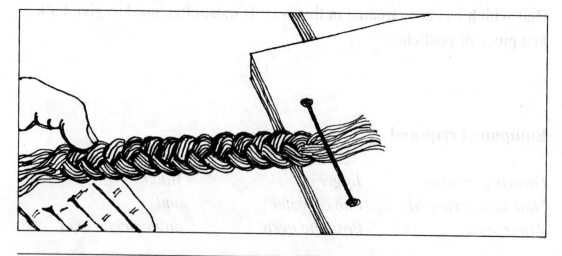

9 'Felt' or tie the point ends. Mark the roots carefully.

10 Repeat processes 3 to 10, until all the hair to be curled has been plaited.

11 Place a pan of water on to boil.

12 When the water is boiling, place the plaited hair in it and boil for 15 to 20 minutes.

13 Remove from the water and drain.

14 Bake in a warm postiche oven for 30 minutes to one hour, ie. until thoroughly dry.

15 Allow to cool, open the plaits and fasten them together in small bundles.

16 Store in a mothproof container until required.

Revision test

Other methods of permanently curling hair

Without referring to the text or to your notes, answer the following:

1 *Why is it necessary to have more than one method of permanently curling hair?*

2 *What is meant by 'felting'?*

3 *Why is felting used?*

4 *Which method would you use on hair under 8cms in length?*

5 *How is the curl formed?*

6 *When crop curling, how do you make the curl permanent?*

7 *How is this shorter hair stored?*

8 *What method would be used on longer hair?*

9 *What result does this give?*

10 *Where would this be used?*

11 *Briefly explain the method of producing this result on long hair.*

12 *How is this hair stored?*

Permanently crimping the hair

This lesson tells how hair is given a permanent crimp. We find out the uses of such hair.

Tools and materials required

Weaving sticks and clamps

Drawing brushes

Parcel string or carpet thread

Scissors

Hair

Pan of water

Postiche oven (optional)

Spend about 30 minutes reading through the theory section.
The sample should only take you about 15 minutes to prepare.

After you have completed the exercise, carry out the test that follows.
This again should take you about 30 minutes.

Where could hair with a crimp be used in wigmaking?

When considering this question, keep in mind the fact that when the crimping process is completed, the hair is very tight - a permanent frizz one might say.

Note down any ideas you might have.

....

....

....

Now let us find out if any of your ideas were right.

1 Hair that is crimped can be used for adding bulk to hairpieces. For example, in switches, part of the hair used when weaving, may be crimped hair. This will give much more shape to the final piece.

2 Crimped hair is ideal when making Afro hairwork, due to its texture and tight curl.

3 Crimped hair is used to pad out hairstyles. This could be by using crepe pads or pompadour rolls (these will be discussed briefly later). Also this type of hair is used to cover frames for the hair.

4 Crimped hair is used frequently in theatrical work. Beards & moustaches are built up on the face with crimped hair.

Did you guess any of the uses of permanently crimped hair?

You did? - then well done.

No? Well, never mind. You are aware now.

Permanently crimped hair is known as crepe hair.
This is easy to remember because of its feel.

The weaving for crepe weft is the only one that is carried out on fine string instead of weaving silk.

Equipment used during this process

Weaving frame   This consists of two clamps which are fixed firmly to the bench approximately 45 cms apart. Into these are placed the weaving sticks. One has three grooves and is placed into the right hand clamp, whilst the left hand stick has a nail/hook, to allow the strings to be hooked on.

Drawing brushes   Used to hold the hair.

Parcel string/carpet thread   This is used instead of weaving silk. Wind the string around the right hand stick. Two strings are required. After winding both strings, tie together and hook over the left hand nail. This forms the weaving frame for crepe weft.

Scissors	Used to cut the strings.
Hair	It is not necessary to use prepared hair (that is, hair which has been sorted into roots and points).
Pan of water	Used to make the crimp permanent.
Postiche oven	Used when drying the hair. Alternatively, this method can be allowed to dry naturally.

A sample of crepe weft is required for your folder.
This sample has to be at least 15cms in length.

Method

1 Prepare your equipment, as listed at the beginning of the lesson.

2 Set up your weaving frame, using two lengths of parcel string or carpet thread. (See previous notes if you cannot remember how to set up the frame.) We will number the bottom string one and the top string two.

3 Place the hair to be woven into the drawing brushes.

4 Make sure you know the degree of crimp that is needed, as this decides the diameter of the section you take. Draw out a section of hair from the brushes.

5 Place the hair into one hand.

A hint at this point is to hold the ends of the hair with which you are working, between the finger and thumb and keep the lower ends of the hair tightly held between the other fingers of that hand.

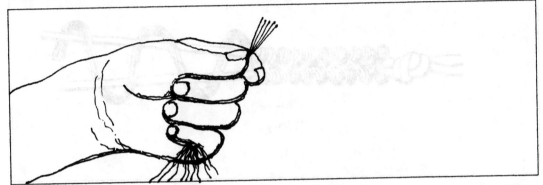

6 Push the hair through the strings from behind. The hair passes between strings one and two.

7 With the other hand, take hold of the hair which is protruding.

8 Take this hair up and over string two.

9 The hair is then passed back between strings one and two - again from back to front.

10 Now take hold of both ends of the hair and twist together.

11 The weaving process is then continued by going under string one. (All the hair is now together and being passed through the strings each time.)

12 Forward from behind, going between strings one and two.

13 Up and over string two.

14 Down, behind string two and forward between strings one and two. The movement is similar to a figure of eight. See the diagram below.

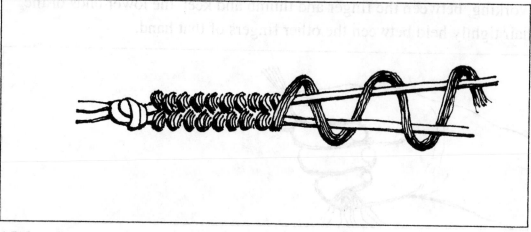

15 Continue in this way until you reach the last 5cms.

16 Take another section of hair and join it to the first by twisting the two pieces of hair together and weaving as before.

17 When all the hair has been used, cut the strings and tie a knot close to the end of the weaving. You will now have a rope of hair.

18 Place this rope into a container, cover with boiling water and allow to boil for 30 minutes.

19 At the end of 30 minutes, carefully remove the rope and allow to dry thoroughly and slowly. This can either be done in a postiche oven or naturally.

Mount your sample into your folder.

When the hair is taken from the strings, it is lightly hackled before use. This makes it expand and go very full.

Revision test on permanently crimping hair

Without referring back to your notes or to the text answer the following on a separate sheet:

1 *What is the name given to permanently crimped hair?*

2 *Give two uses of this hair.*

3 *What is the main difference between the setting up of the weaving frame for this type of weft and for other wefts?*

4 *How far apart are the sticks placed?*

5 *What type of thread is used in the making of crepe weft?*

6 *What is the difference between hair that can be used for crimping and hair used for other wefts?*

7 *Which stick has three grooves?*

8 *How are the strings numbered?*

9 *Draw a diagram of the weaving frame and number the strings.*

10 *What determines the degree of crimp achieved?*

11 *Why are drawing brushes used?*

12 *What does the weaving for crepe weft resemble?*

13 *Briefly describe the weaving process.*

14 *Once all the hair has been woven, how is it given its permanent crimp?*

15 *How is the prepared hair made ready for use?*

Crepe pads and pompadour rolls

As we stated earlier one of the uses of crepe hair is in the making of crepe pads and pompadour rolls.

Equipment required

Drawing brushes	*Weaving sticks and clamps*
Hackle	*Needle and cotton to match the hair colour*
Clamp	
	Tissue paper
Crepe hair	
	Postiche oven
Carpet thread to match hair colour	

Crepe pads

Crepe pads can be used on their own or in twos or threes. They are positioned inside a style - for example, to fill out the top of a 'pony tail'.

Method

1 Prepare all equipment.

2 Set up the weaving frame, using two lengths of carpet thread that matches the hair colour.

3 Clamp the hackle to the bench.

4 Cut the thread from a length of crepe hair.

5 Gently loosen the hair with the fingers.

6 Hackle the crepe hair. It will become full and fluffy.

7 Place this hackled hair into the drawing brushes.

8 Cover the hackle for safety.
Alternatively, the hair can be left in the hackle, providing one of the drawing brushes is placed on top during working.

9 The first weaving is that for the loop.
This is done by taking a fine mesh of the crepe hair and weaving in fine crepe weft. 3 to 5cms are required for the loop.

Try to fill in the diagram of the
weaving for crepe weft.

Did you remember to twist the
ends together after the first turn?

If you were at all uncertain, then
check back in your notes at this
point.

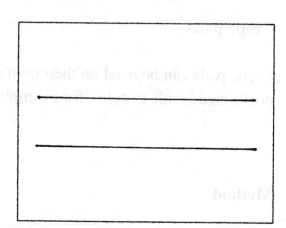

10 After the weaving for the loop has been completed, the bulk of the
pad is made.

11 Fairly thick meshes of hair are taken.

12 Weave in and out of the threads to form an 'M'.

13 Leave the hair equal on each
side before sliding up to the
previous weaving. Thus the
weaving is carried out in the centre
of the hair.

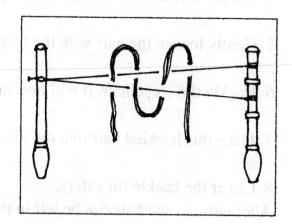

14 Next, take another fairly thick
mesh of hair, but this time
weave a 'W'.

15 Start at the top - pass behind the top thread.

16 The hair is then passed through the centre of the two threads.

17 Take the hair under the bottom thread and back between the two threads, moving back upwards.

18 Proceed to take the hair up and over the top.

19 Bring the hair forwards between the two threads.

20 The hair is taken under the bottom thread again and then back upwards between the two threads.

21 Tighten the hair, leaving the weaving in the centre of the mesh of hair.

22 Slide along to join the previous weaving.

23 The amount of weaving that should be carried out depends on the size required.
As a general rule the length of weaving should be two thirds of the required finished pad.
Example: A pad which is required to be 15cms in length needs approximately 10cms of weft.

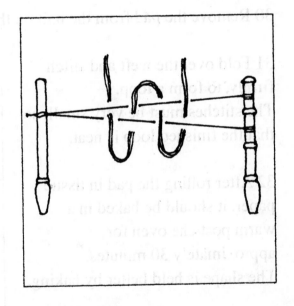

24 Measure your weaving and as you come to the end, make your last 'M' & 'W' much finer than the others. It makes the work much firmer.

25 The final mesh should be woven as a finishing knot for two string fly weft.

26 Cut the carpet thread and tie a fine knot close to the finishing level.

27 Allow it to hang from the nail in the left hand stick.

28 Using the palms of the hands, roll the hair, to shape it into a well-rounded pad. The hair will blend together due to its texture.

29 Once the pad is to the correct shape, any fine fly-away bits of hair that might be standing away from the pad may be trimmed off.

NB Only the very ends should be trimmed.

30 Remove the pad from the nail on the left hand pad.

31 Fold over the weft and stitch firmly, to form a loop.
The stitches must be very small, so that the finished loop is neat.

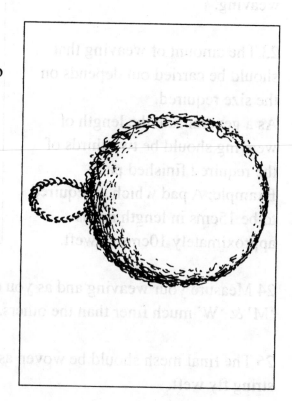

32 After rolling the pad in tissue paper, it should be baked in a warm postiche oven for approximately 30 minutes.
The shape is held better by baking.

33 Allow the pad to cool.

34 Store, wrapped in its tissue paper, in a mothproof container until required.

Pompadour rolls

The pompadour roll is similar to the crepe pad except that it has two loops. Because of these loops, the pompadour roll can be gripped on the crown area, or similar and the client's own hair is dressed over the top. As its name suggests, the pompadour roll can be pinned just behind the front hairline to give a pompadour style when the lady's hair is dressed over, thereby giving height and bulk to a style.

Method

1 Prepare all equipment.

2 Set up the weaving frame, using two lengths of carpet thread that matches the hair colour.

3 Clamp the hackle to the bench.

4 Hackle the crepe hair, as before, until it becomes full and fluffy.

5 Place the hackled hair into the drawing brushes or hackle and drawing brush.

6 Cover the hackle for safety, when not in use.

7 Weave the loop in fine crepe weaving, approximately 3 to 5cms

8 Next, weave the bulk of the pad.

9 As before, fairly thick meshes of hair are taken and woven in 'M's and 'W's.

10 Tighten the hair, leaving the weaving in the centre of the mesh of hair, after each 'M' & 'W'.

11 Slide along to join the previous weaving.

12 The amount of weaving that should be carried out depends on the size required, the same as for the crepe pad.

13 Make your last 'M' & 'W' much finer than the others. It makes the work much firmer.

14 The final weft should be made as a finishing knot for two string fly weft.

15 Whilst the weaving is still securely attached to the weaving frame, gently roll and shape, moulding the hair over to the right slightly.

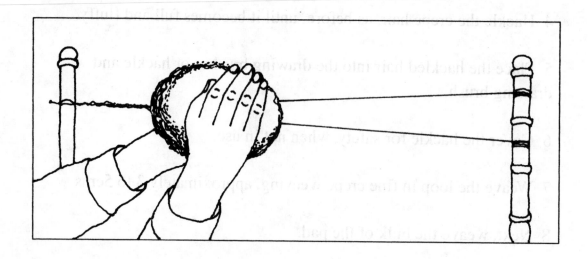

16 Using these fine ends, begin weaving, in fine crepe weft, to form the loop at the other end.

17 Add fine meshes of crepe hair to the weaving as you progress, until 3 to 5 cms have been completed.

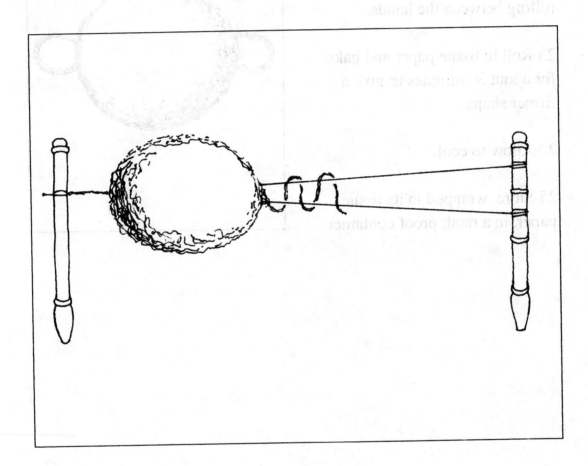

18 Next, cut down from the right hand stick.

19 Tie a very fine knot.

20 Remove from the left hand stick.

21 Fold each end over, to form its loop and stitch, using very fine stitches.

22 Re-establish the shape by rolling between the hands.

23 Roll in tissue paper and bake for about 30 minutes to give a firmer shape.

24 Allow to cool.

25 Store, wrapped in its tissue paper, in a moth proof container.

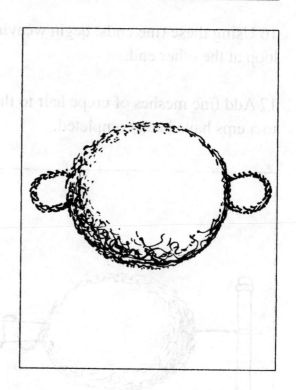

Different types of weaving

This lesson shows you the various methods of weaving and their uses.
You will learn how to weave hair.
You will also learn about the different types of weft and their uses.

The theory section should take only about 15 minutes.
The revision test should take no more than 15 minutes.

Allowing time to try out the weaving before making your finished sample, one and a half hours should be enough for the practical work.

Different types of weaving

What is meant by weaving in relation to wigmaking?
It is the art of weaving hair onto strings before it is made into postiche.

How are the various hairpieces made?

There are three main methods:

1 By winding the weft around a central stem.

2 By folding or stitching into different shapes.

3 By stitching onto a foundation as in weft wigs or in hair ornamentation.

Different wefts

Once-in weaving	Also known as flat weft. Forms the bulk of all postiche work.
Twice in weaving	The hair is given an extra turn.
Thrice in weaving	Once again, an extra turn is used. Used in the making of weft wigs.
Two string fly weft & three string fly weft	Used to give a fine neat finish to most hair

Why do we have different types of weaving?

To give different finishes.

The choice of weft is made after deciding upon the thickness required for the finished hairpiece. The type of hairpiece, itself, also determines the method used.

76

Tools and equipment used when weaving

A pair of clamps	Firmly attached to the bench. These hold the weaving sticks.
Weaving sticks	One plain with a nail, the other grooved. These hold the weaving silk.
Weaving silk	Used in a colour to match the hair to be used. The hair is woven onto this silk.
Paper	The weaving silk is attached to the paper before it is wound onto the sticks. This allows the operator to tighten or slacken the silks as needed.
Drawing brushes	Used to hold the hair. The brushes must be kept clean.
Bees' wax	Used to strengthen and preserve the silks.
Jockey/clip	Holds the weaving in place as you progress. (Use a silver clip.)
Hair	This is hair which has been previously prepared.

What can you remember about setting up the weaving frame?

....

....

....

The weaving you are going to carry out during this lesson requires the weaving frame to have three lengths of weaving silk.

The weaving frame

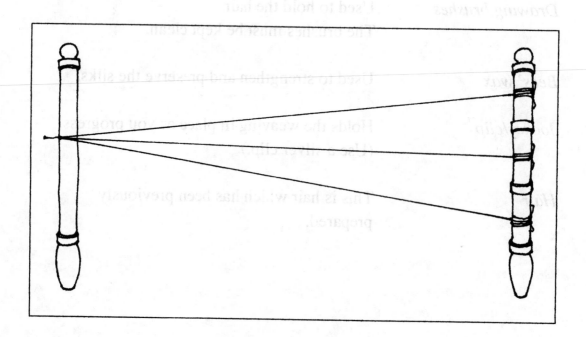

Fly weft

This method of weaving is so called because, when it is finished, the roots fly away, leaving a very fine, neat finish to the work.

Method

1 Prepare all your equipment as listed at the beginning.

2 Set up the weaving frame, numbering the silks from the bottom.

3 Place the prepared hair into the drawing brushes.

4 Draw off a fine section of hair.

5 Hold in one hand.
Can you remember the best way of holding the hair?

....

....

If you cannot remember, then check back in the text to the section about crepe weft

6 Holding the points firmly between the lower fingers, bring the roots of the hair through, from back to front, between silks one and two.

7 Take the roots in the other hand.
NB Do not release the hair already held.

8 Bring the roots up and over the top of silk three.

9 The roots are now pushed forward between silks three and two.

10 Next, take the roots right down and under the bottom silk, number one.

11 Take the roots up behind silks one and two, then bring them forward between silks two and three.

12 Take the roots over the top of silk three and bring them back from behind, passing between silks three and two.

13 Hold both ends of the hair down from the silks. (The hair is woven in and out of the silks.)

14 Gently draw the hair that is held in the left hand (these are the points) downwards to shorten the roots held in the right hand to about 3cms.

15 Carefully tighten the weaving on the silks.

16 Slide the weaving close to the previously woven hair.

17 Place the jockey/clip close to the weft, to prevent it from coming undone.

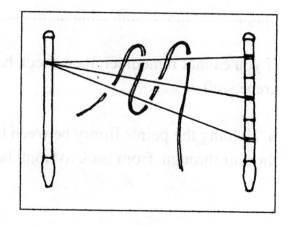

Once in weaving

This is the method used for most hair work.
It is also known as flat weft.

Method

1 Prepare all your equipment as listed at the beginning.

2 Set up the weaving frame, numbering the silks from the bottom.

3 Place the prepared hair into the drawing brushes.

4 Draw off a fine section of hair.

5 Hold in one hand.

6 Holding the points firmly between the lower fingers, bring the roots of the hair through, from back to front, between silks one and two.

7 Take the roots in the other hand.
NB Do not release the hair already held.

8 Bring the roots up and over the top of silk three.

9 The roots are now pushed forward between silks three and two.

10 Next, take the roots right down and under the bottom silk, number one.

11 Take the roots up behind silks one and two, then bring them forward between silks two and three.

12 Take the roots over the top of silk three and bring them back from behind, passing between silks three and two.

13 Push the roots to the back, passing between silks two and one.

14 Hold both ends of the hair down from the silks. (The hair is woven in and out of the silks.)

15 Gently draw the hair that is held in the left hand (these are the points) downwards to shorten the roots held in the right hand to about 3cms.

16 Carefully tighten the weaving on the silks.

17 Slide the weaving close to the previously woven hair.

18 Place the jockey/clip close to the weft, to prevent it from coming undone.

In order to ensure that the weaving remains in position on the silks, we have to weave a starting knot, before weaving commences and a finishing knot, when the required length has been completed.

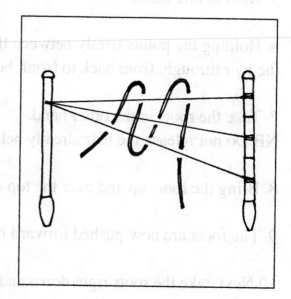

The starting knot

Method

1 Take a fine section of hair and weave, as for once in weaving, up to number 12.

2 Take the points that are held in the left hand across the front of the weaving and push them through to the back, going between silks two and one.

3 Gently pull down on the points to shorten the roots (right hand).

4 Tighten the hair on the silks.

5 Hold firmly in position, using the jockey.

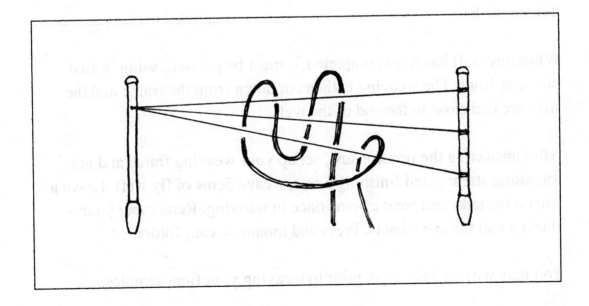

The finishing knot

Method

1 Take a fine section of hair and weave, as for flyweft, up to number 12.

2 Take the roots which are held in the right hand, across the front of the work.

3 Pass the roots through to the back, going between silks two and one, at the left hand side of your work.

4 Gently pull down the points to tighten the hair.

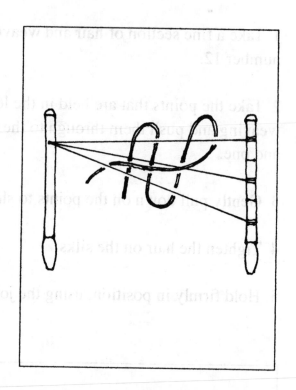

When any weft has been completed, it must be pressed, using heated pinching irons. The weaving is then cut down from the frame and the silks are tied close to the end of the weft.

After answering the revision test, set up your weaving frame and not forgetting starting and finishing knots, weave 5cms of fly weft. Leave a gap on the silks and weave 5cms once in weaving. Remember your starting and finishing knots. Press and mount in your folder.

You may wish to have a go, prior to weaving your final samples.

Twice in weaving

Another name for twice in weaving is medium weft because it is a little thicker than once in weaving but not as thick as thrice in weaving.
As its name suggests, it is carried out in the same manner as once in weaving with an extra turn.

Method

1 Prepare all your equipment.

2 Set up the weaving frame, numbering as before.

3 Place the prepared hair into the drawing brushes.

4 Draw off a fine section of hair.

5 Hold in one hand.

6 Holding the points firmly between the lower fingers, bring the roots of the hair through, from back to front, between silks 1 & 2.

7 Take the roots in the other hand.
NB Do not release the hair already held.

8 Bring the roots up and over the top of silk 3.

9 The roots are now pushed forward between silks 3 & 2.

10 Next, take the roots right down and under the bottom silk, number 1.

11 Take the roots up behind silks 1 & 2, then bring them forward between silks 2 & 3.

12 Take the roots over the top of silk 3 and bring them back from behind, passing between silks 3 & 2.

13 The roots are once again taken right down and under the bottom silk, number 1.

14 The roots are taken up behind silks 1 & 2, bringing them forward between silks 2 & 3.

15 Push the roots to the back, passing them between silks 2 & 1.

16 Hold both ends of the hair down from the silks. (The hair is woven in and out of the silks.)

17 Gently draw the hair that is held in the left hand (these are the points), downwards, to shorten the roots held in the right hand to about 3cms.

18 Tighten the weaving on the silks.

19 Slide along, until it sits close to the previously woven hair.

20 Use a jockey to hold into position.

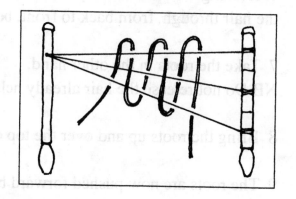

Thrice in weaving

Again, this type of weaving is carried out as for once in weaving, but has two extra turns.
This is also known as wig weft, as it is the method for a weft made wig.
Between twenty five and thirty metres of weft are required for a full wig.

Method

1 Prepare all your equipment.

2 Set up the weaving frame, numbering as before.

3 Place the prepared hair into the drawing brushes.

4 Draw off a fine section of hair.

5 Hold in one hand.

6 Holding the points firmly between the lower fingers, bring the roots of the hair through, from back to front, between silks 1 & 2.

7 Take the roots in the other hand.
NB Do not release the hair already held.

8 Bring the roots up and over the top of silk 3.

9 The roots are now pushed forward between silks 3 & 2.

10 Next, take the roots right down and under the bottom silk, number 1.

11 Take the roots up behind silks 1 & 2 then bring them forward between silks 2 & 3.

12 Take the roots over the top of silk 3 and bring them back from behind, passing between silks 3 & 2.

13 The roots are once again taken right down and under the bottom silk, number 1.

14 The roots are taken up behind silks 1 & 2, bringing them forward between silks 2 & 3.

15 The roots are once again taken right down and under the bottom silk, number 1.

16 The roots are taken up behind silks 1 & 2, bringing them forward between silks 2 & 3. Over silk 3 and forward between 3 & 2.

17 Push the roots to the back, passing them between silks 2 & 1.

18 Hold both ends of the hair down from the silks. (The hair is woven in and out the silks.)

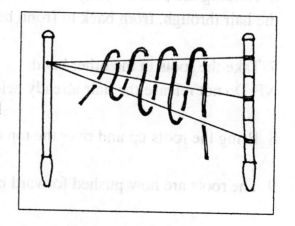

19 Gently draw the hair that is held in the left hand (these are the points), downwards, to shorten the roots held in the right hand to about 3cms.

20 Tighten the weaving on the silks.

21 Slide along, until it sits close to the previously woven hair.

22 Use a jockey to hold into position.

Two string fly weft

The finest of all the wefts, it gives a very fine finish to postiche like pincurls, marteau and double loop clusters.
As three string fly weft is also called top row, two string fly weft can be termed top row.

Method

1 Prepare all equipment.

2 Place the hair to be woven, into the drawing brushes.

3 Set up the weaving frame.

4 Release the bottom silk, no 1 and allow it to hang loosely.

5 Draw off a fine section of hair.

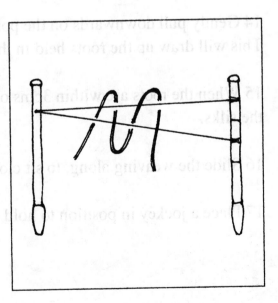

6 Hold the roots firmly between the lower fingers.

7 Bring the roots forward between silks 2 & 3. Remember not to release

....

8 Take the hair up and over the top of silk 3.

9 Pass the hair behind the silks and forward between silks 3 & 2.

10 Allow the hair to go under silk 2, then up behind silk 2.

11 Let the hair come forward between silks 2 & 3, as before.

12 It is next taken over silk three, to pass from back to front between silks 3 & 2.

13 Hold both ends of hair downwards.

14 Gently pull downwards on the points which are held in the left hand. This will draw up the roots held in the left hand.

15 When the roots are within 3cms of the silks, tighten the weaving on the silks.

16 Slide the weaving along, to sit close to the previously woven hair.

17 Place a jockey in position to hold the hair.

Two string fly weft has its own starting knot.
This diagram shows how the hair is woven as for two string fly weft and how the points are then brought across the front and pushed back between silks 2 & 3.

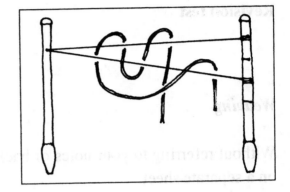

The only time a finishing knot is required for two string fly weft, is when it is used for a double loop cluster. The adjacent diagram shows how the hair is woven as for two string fly weft. The roots are then passed from right to left and back between silks 2 & 3.

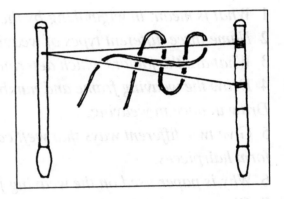

More often, though, two string fly weft is used at the beginning of the weaving. Where this is the case, the bottom silk that had been released is tightened up again. The chosen method of weaving is then carried straight on. There is no necessity for a starting knot between flyweft and the bulk of the weaving. One simply follows the other.

Revision test

Weaving

Without referring to your notes or back in the text, answer the following on a separate sheet.

1 *What is meant in wigmaking by the term weaving?*
2 *Name three different types of weaving.*
3 *What are the factors which determine the weft used?*
4 *Draw the weaving frame and number the silks.*
Draw in once in weaving.
5 *Give two different ways that weft can be stitched up to form hairpieces.*
6 *Why is paper used on the weaving frame?*
7 *Give one use of bees' wax.*
8 *What is a jockey and why is it used?*
9 *Draw a pair of drawing brushes correctly holding the hair.*
Label.
10 *Draw diagrams for the following.*
a The starting knot b The finishing knot c Once in weaving d Three string flyweft
Number the silks and indicate the roots and the points.
11 *Why are starting and finishing knots important?*
12 *Name two processes carried out when weaving has been completed.*

How did you manage the test?
Do you feel confident to carry out the weaving?
It might be advisable to keep your diagrams handy whilst
you are working.

The diamond mesh

This lesson and the one that follows, demonstrate two different ways of using the weaving you have learned. They also use two totally different methods of sewing up.

The theory part of this lesson should take no more than 15 minutes to read through.
The revision test should take about 15 minutes maximum.
The practical aspect of the lesson will take several hours.
I suggest that you work for about one hour at a time.
By having a break your work will grow much quicker.

The diamond mesh

The diamond mesh uses wired weft.

What is wired weft?
Wired weft is made by exchanging the middle silk, number 2, for a
fine wire.
This wire gives a certain amount of rigidity to the weft when it
is completed.
The use of wired weft is to make a hairpiece with a flexible base.
This base can be moulded to fit the contours of the head at the point it is
being worn.
Pieces made of wired weft are normally worn on the crown area to give
height to the final hairstyle.
After the weaving has been completed it is moulded and stitched into a
pattern, which, when opened out for use, resembles diamonds.

Therefore the diamond mesh is a piece of postiche made from wired weft
and worn normally on the crown of the head.

The diamond mesh uses one type of weaving only. It is the one which is
also called flat weft.

Which one is it?

....

Equipment used for wired weft

Weaving frame   Set up the weaving frame, as before, but
                           replace the centre silk with wire.

Drawing brushes   Used to hold the hair.

Needle and sewing silk   For the sewing up.
                           The silk should match the hair being used.

Scissors   For cutting the silks.

Pinching irons   Heated, then used to press the weaving.

Jockey/clip   Used to hold the weft whilst weaving.

Weaving silk   To form the weaving frame.
&
weaving wire

Bees' wax   To protect the silks.

Hair   Prepared hair for weaving.

Faults that can happen and how to avoid them

Weaving uneven and untidy

Make sure that each section you take is of the same thickness.
Ensure the silks and central wire have an even tension.
Correct tightening of the hair on the silks.

Insufficient weft to make desired piece

Draw an exact pattern, that is to scale.
Decide on the shape of base required, then take careful measurements.
Take care to measure the points before sewing.

Preparation

Draw a diagram of the base to scale.
Work out the exact amount of weft you need. Remember a minimum of 100cms is needed.
This pattern will sit side by side with your sample, in your folder.

Method

1 Prepare all the equipment, as listed at the beginning.

2 Prepare your pattern.

3 Set up the weaving frame, using two lengths of silk and one length of wire.

4 Place the hair into the drawing brushes -?- protruding.

5 Carry out a starting knot.

6 Check the amount of weaving required.

7 Weave the necessary amount in moderately fine, once in weaving.

8 Carry out a finishing knot.

9 Press and cut down from the frame.

10 Turn the wire in at both ends.

11 Form the shape of the piece against your pattern.

12 Sew into the desired shape, using thread of a matching colour.
The stitches should be small and neat.

13 Make provision for attaching the piece to the head.
This may be in the form of a 'cache peigne' (hidden comb), or by loops.
Dress the finished hairpiece.

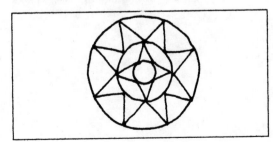

Revision test

The diamond mesh

Without referring to your notes or to the text, answer the following on a separate sheet.

1 *What do we mean by wired weft?*
2 *What are the benefits of wired weft?*
3 *Where is a diamond mesh usually worn?*
4 *Why is this piece called a diamond mesh?*
5 *Wired weft uses one type of weaving only. What is it?*
6 *What is its other name?*
7 *Give three items of equipment that are used when making wired weft.*
8 *Give two faults that can occur when weaving.*
9 *Explain how to avoid one of those faults.*
10 *How do you ensure that you will have enough weft?*
11 *What type of sewing silk should be used?*
12 *What sort of stitching is used when sewing up a diamond?*
13 *What is a 'cache peigne'?*
14 *What is a 'cache peigne' used for?*

The two stem switch

This lesson deals with a hairpiece of a different type.
You will learn another method of putting a piece together.
The formation and sewing up are completely different from the
diamond mesh.

Take about 15 - 20 minutes each on the theory and the revision test.
Your practical work will take two to two and a half hours.

This lesson deals with the making of a hairpiece which is sewn up onto a central stem.

Why a two stem switch?

Switches can be of one, two or three stems.
A single stem switch can be used to add bulk to a finished dressing.
A two stem switch can be coiled and wound around the head.
It can be used to add additional bulk to a hairstyle.
A three stem switch can be plaited in addition to the above.

In each case the preparation and procedure are the same except for the number of stems woven and sewn up.

Equipment used in the making of a two stem switch

Weaving frame	Three lengths of weaving silk are required.
Drawing brushes	Used to hold...
Needle and sewing silk	Used for the sewing up.
	The silk should..
	....
Pinching irons	Heated, then used for..
	....

................................/clip   Holds the hair whilst weaving.

Weaving silk   Used on the weaving frame.

...........................*wax*   ....the silks.

Hair   ....hair must be used.

Winding machine   Also called the twisting or turning machine.
Assists when spirally winding the weft when sewing up.

Tail cord   Used in conjunction with the twisting/winding machine.
The tail cord forms the stem of the piece,

The two stem switch uses both fly weft and once in weaving.

A sample two stem switch is required for your folder.
Each stem to be a minimum of 7cms in length.
I would advise the weaving for each stem to be 20cms.

Method

1 Prepare all the equipment listed at the beginning.

2 Place the longest hair into the drawing brushes. This is for the fly weft. There should be just enough to weave 5cms.

3 Divide the remaining hair into two equal portions. (It is often easier to carry out this dividing, after the fly weft has been woven.)

4 Set up the weaving frame. Use three lengths of weaving silk.

5 Wind 15cms of clear silk onto the left hand stick.

6 Make a starting knot.

7 Weave 5cms flyweft. This must be very fine and neat as it will form the outside of your hairpiece. Use the longest hair for this weaving.

8 If you have not already done so, divide the remaining hair into two equal portions.
Place one of these into the brushes.

9 *Without* leaving a space, weave this portion of hair in moderately fine once in weaving.

10 Finish with a finishing knot.

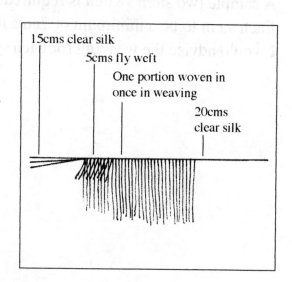

15cms clear silk

5cms fly weft

One portion woven in once in weaving

20cms clear silk

11 You have now completed the first stem and the fly weft. Wind these onto the left hand stick along with a further 15/20cms of clear silk.

12 Place the second portion of hair into the brushes.

13 Make a starting knot.

14 Weave the portion of hair in moderately fine once in weaving only.

15 Finish with a finishing knot.

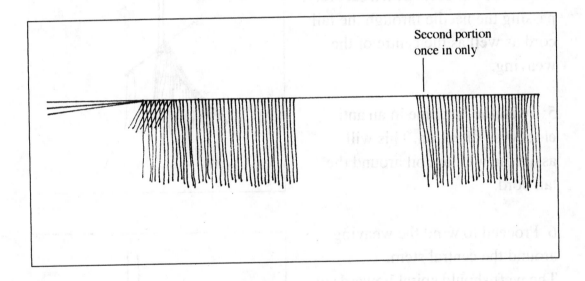

Second portion once in only

16 Heat the pinching irons.

17 Press the hairwork over tissue paper.

18 Cut down. The cut should be made at a point 5cms from the finishing knot end.

19 Tie at the finishing knot end only.

Winding a two stem switch

1 Prepare the winding/twisting machine with tail cord.

2 Fix the machine to the bench/table.

3 Thread a needle with sewing silk which matches the hair used.

4 Attach the second stem woven, approximately 1.25cms from the end of the tail cord. Stitch securely, passing the needle through the tail cord as well as the centre of the weaving.

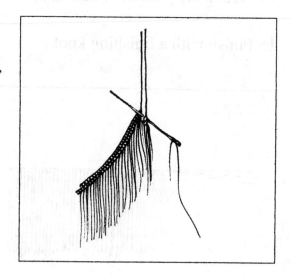

5 Twist the machine in an anti-clockwise direction. This will assist the weft to coil around the tail cord.

6 Proceed to wind the weaving around the central stem.
The weft should spiral upwards at each turn.

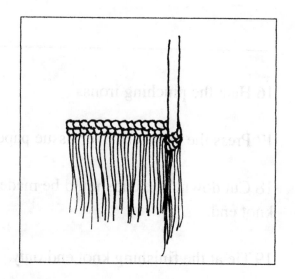

7 Stitch securely at intervals, as the winding continues.

8 The weft will slide along the silks slightly. This was the reason for leaving clear silk at the

beginning of each stem and also why we did not tie a knot at the beginning of each stem.

9 When all the weft in this second stem has been stitched, fasten off securely, by sewing several times.

10 Cut this stem from the twisting/winding machine, at a point about 2cms up the tail cord.

11 Take the other piece of weft (that is the one you wove first of all - the one with the flyweft attached).

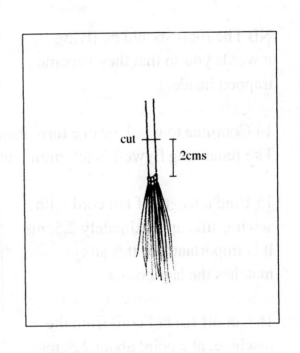

12 Wind this first stem exactly the same way that you wound the other stem, but only as far as the fly weft.

Therefore, you attach the

....

knot end of the weaving to
the tail cord

..........................cms up.

Wind around the cord stitching

....

13 When the fly weft is reached, attach the other stem to this stem by placing the tail cords side by side and stitching through both stems securely.

NB The roots should be flying towards you so that they become trapped inside.

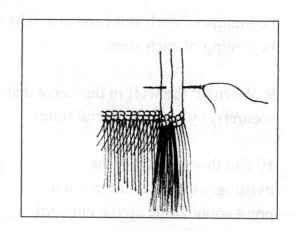

14 Continue to wind for one turn, using about 1.25cms of the flyweft. The remaining flyweft is left until later.

15 Bind a length of tail cord with sewing silk, approximately 2.5cms. It is important that this silk matches the hair colour.

16 Cut off the tail cord from the machine, at a point about 2.5cms up the cord.

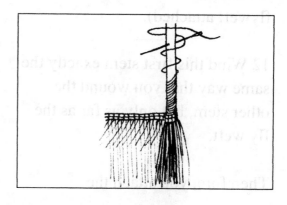

17 Fold this cord over, to form a loop and stitch securely.

18 Tie the loop back to the machine.

19 Wind the remaining weft around the loop, stitching securely as you do so.

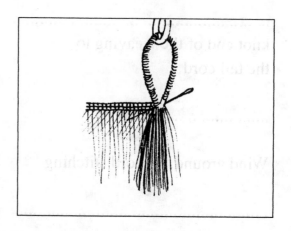

20 Finish off the top, by running the sewing silk around to form a silk cap.

21 Press the switch using heated pinching irons and under tissue paper.

22 Dress the switch as required.

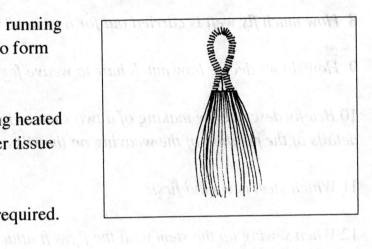

Revision test on the making of a switch

Without referring back to your notes or to the text, answer the following on a separate sheet:

1 *How would you describe a switch?*

2 *Up to how many stems can a switch have?*

3 *Give the use of one of those switches.*

4 *What types of weaving are used in the making of a switch?*

5 *What is the name given to the machine used in the sewing up procedure?*

6 *What is the name given to the cord used with the machine?*

7 *Which hair is used for the fly weft?*

8 *How much fly weft is carried out for a switch?*

9 *How do we decide how much hair to weave for each stem?*

10 *Briefly describe the making of a two stem switch. Make sure you give details of the position of the weaving on the silks.*

11 *Which stem is wound first?*

12 *When sewing up the stem with the flyweft attached, how far do we stitch to begin with?*

13 *When putting both stems together, what must we be sure of doing?*

14 *How is the loop formed?*

15 *What is the name given to the covering between the loop and the hair at the top of the switch?*

Small pieces of postiche

In this section, you will learn how to make smaller pieces of postiche which are used to add a single curl.

Equipment required

Weaving sticks and clamps

Weaving silk

Jockey

Drawing brushes

Hair to be woven

Pinching irons

Tissue paper

Scissors

Needle

Thread to match the hair colour

Pinwire

Pliers

Pincurls

As stated on the previous page, there are smaller pieces of postiche which are designed to add a single curl or wave.

Benefits of this type of postiche

1 May be used on the forehead to produce a fringe effect without the necessity to cut the hair.

2 They can be used to increase the bulk of the hair at a particular position in a style.

3 They can be used to give flashes of colour.

There are three different pincurls

The ordinary pincurl	The smallest pincurl
The pinwave	A little larger
The pincurl marteau	The largest pincurl

To differentiate between them, it is easiest to remember that a pincurl is wound round a pinwire, a pin wave is stitched flat and the pincurl marteau is a combination of the two.

The ordinary pincurl

Method

1 Set up the weaving frame using three lengths of

....

Draw a diagram of the weaving frame and number the silks

Did you remember to number from the bottom up?

Good.

2 Next, place the hair into the drawing brushes with the roots facing towards you.

If I state that the bottom silk is now loosened and allowed to drop down a little, which method of weaving does that suggest?

Two string fly weft, yes.

Fill in the movements for two string fly weft below.

2cms of this top row are required. The weaving should be very fine.

What must you begin with?

3 After completing 2cms of two string fly weft, tighten the bottom silk up again.

4 Continue weaving, this time in once in weaving, for a further 8cms.

5 Finish with a finishing knot.

Can you recall what must be done next?

....

....

....

Did you get it right?

6 The answer is to press with heated pinching irons.
Cover the weaving with tissue paper first.

7 Cut the weaving down from the sticks and tie a knot close to the weaving at each end.

8 Take a pinwire, which is sometimes referred to as an Italian pin. This is a thin length of soft wire rather like a roller pin.

9 Using a pair of pliers, turn the very ends up.

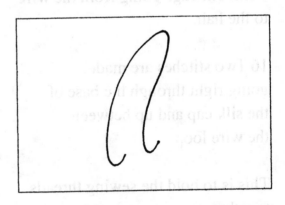

10 Hook this loop into the weaving at the finishing knot end.

11 Thread a needle with a length of a silk to match the hair colour.

12 Begin stitching the pincurl, working through the centre of the weft and the pin wire.

13 Continue sewing whilst you wind the weft spirally up the pin wire.

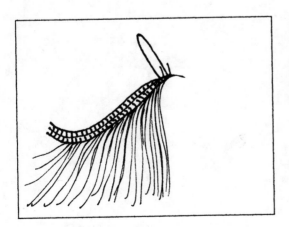

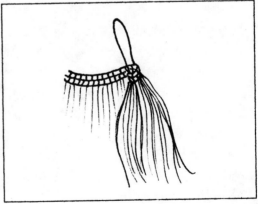

14 When all the weft has been stitched securely to the pinwire, carry out two last stitches to make it firm.

15 The pincurl is finished off with a silk cap.

The sewing thread is wound around and around so that there is a smooth edge going from the wire to the hair.

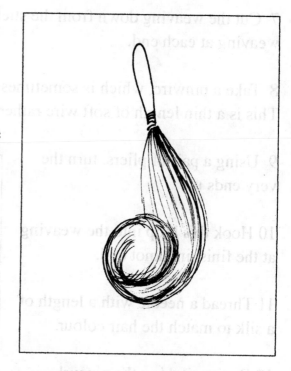

16 Two stitches are made, going right through the base of the silk cap and up between the wire loop.

This is to hold the sewing threads together.

17 Press the cap between heated pinching irons.

Cover with tissue paper first.

The Pinwave

The pinwave has the same amount and type of weaving as the ordinary pincurl. See if you can fill in the gaps without looking back.

2cms ....

....weaving.

The difference is in the sewing up.

Method

I will assume that you have already carried out the necessary weaving.

1 Press the weaving with heated pinching irons over tissue paper.

2 Cut down from the frame and tie a knot, close to the weaving at each end.

3 Fold over, at the finishing knot end, a portion of the weaving approximately 2cms long.

4 Stitch, by passing the needle through the centre of the weaving, folded over and under the weft at the back.

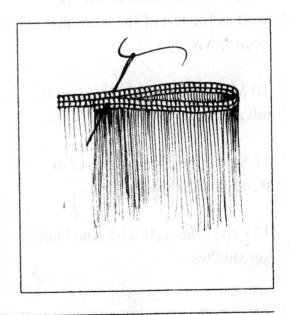

5 Bring the needle back, passing it through the centre of the back weft and over the top of the bottom weft.

This means that you are stitching the top of the bottom weft to the bottom of the top weft.

6 Fold over again.
This fold should be slightly less than 2cms.

7 Stitch as before. If you have sewn it correctly, then your weft will be advancing upwards each turn.

8 Continue in the same way until you reach the fly weft. The width should now be down to 1cm.

9 Sew the first fold of the fly weft as the rest of the weft has been sewn.

10 Make the last fold level, not advancing.

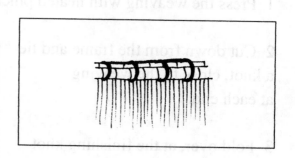

11 Sew either over and over or through and through.

12 Cover the weft with fine blanket stitches.

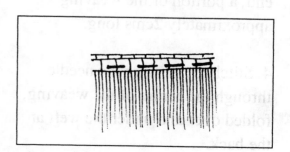

13 Finish by making a loop. Six loops of silk are made from one side to the other. These are then buttonholed over.

14 Cover with tissue paper and press with heated pressing irons.

The Pincurl Marteau

The largest of the pincurls, it is a combination of the two others.
The pincurl marteau requires 2cms of two string fly weft and 14 to 16 cms of once in weaving. After the weft has been pressed and cut down, it is sewn up as follows.

Sewing up a pincurl marteau

1 Fold over 3cms at the finishing knot end and sew as for a pinwave.

2 Make four folds, decreasing each time and sewing as for the pinwave.

The weft will advance slightly as you sew.

Try to make your weft decrease to 1cm wide.

3 Take a pin wire and hook the ends up using pliers.

4 Hook this into the centre of the 1cm width of weaving.

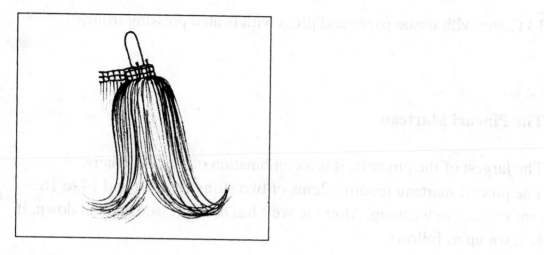

5 Finish sewing the weft, but now as if you were stitching the ordinary pincurl.

6 Press as before

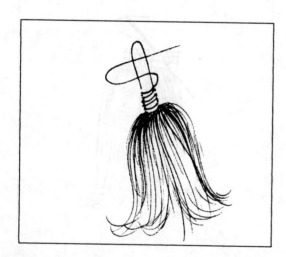

The Marteau

I shall explain in this section the making of a marteau and its uses.

Equipment required

Weaving sticks and clamps

Weaving silk

Hair to be woven

Drawing brushes

Pinching irons

Tissue paper

Scissors

Needle

Thread to match hair colour

Postiche comb or clip

The Marteau

This is a piece of postiche made from weft which is stitched up flat.

Where can the marteau be worn?

1 At the nape of the neck, to lengthen short nape hair.

2 On its side, in a cluster of curls down the back of the head.

3 Two or more stitched together can be worn as a chignon.

4 Two stitched together can be worn with the join forming a centre parting, making the hair appear all one length - sometimes called a swathe.

Possibly, the hardest part of the marteau is understanding how to work out the amount of weaving required.

It can be broken down into quite simple areas.

First of all, one must decide on the length required for the finished postiche.

If, for example, the marteau is going to be worn at the nape area of a hairstyle, then the width of the nape area will need to be measured.

Take this measurement and double it.

Add to this figure 1cm, to allow for the amount taken up in the turn.

You now have the amount of fly weft required.

Next, we take the measurement and multiply it by the number of folds that are required in the final piece.

This is where the problems tend to occur.

A marteau can have as many folds as you wish.

The more folds there are, the longer the inner base will be.

Again, when you have your final figure you add to it, to allow for the turnings. This time 2cms are allowed.

Example - for a 12cm marteau.

If three turns are decided upon, the amount of weaving required will be:

Fly weft	$24 + 1 = 25$cms
and	
Once in weaving	$36 + 2 = 38$cms

If five turns are decided upon, the amount of weaving will be:

Fly weft	$24 + 1 = 25$cms
and	
Once in weaving	$60 + 2 = 62$cms

To summarise:

A marteau requires twice the final width plus one of flyweft and a number of turns (decided upon by the desired result) plus two of once in weaving.

Method

1 Set up the weaving frame, using three lengths of weaving silk.

2 Place the hair to be woven into the drawing brushes.

3 Loosen the bottom silk and weave the required amount of two string fly weft.

What must be carried out before weaving is begun?

....

4 Without leaving a gap, continue in once in weaving for the amount needed.

Fill in the weaving movements for two string fly weft and once in weaving.

122

5 Press the weaving with heated pinching irons over tissue paper.

6 Cut down and tie a knot close to the ends of the weaving.

7 Make the first fold at the finishing knot end, just slightly less than the desired finished length.

8 Allow the weft behind to be a little above the folded weft.

9 Sew by passing the needle through the centre of the lower weft and letting it come out under the weft at the back.

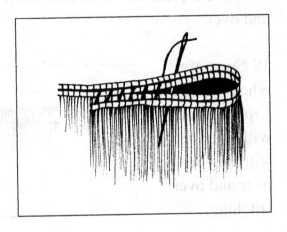

10 Now bring the needle back through the centre of the top weft and over the top of the lower weft (See diagram on page 117).

11 Continue stitching in this manner until the other end is reached.

12 Make another fold so the stitching just carried out is hidden. This fold should be just a little longer.

13 Allow this weft to be above the other so that it fits closely together.

14 Stitch as before. The needle will pass through the centre of the lower weft (the one which was the top weft last time) and out under the back weft.

15 Bring the needle back through the centre of the top weft and over the top of the lower weft.

16 Continue folding, each fold a little longer than the last until half the fly weft has been sewn in this manner.
It should now have increased in width to the length required for the finished marteau.

17 Make the last fold level and stitch either through and through or over and over.

18 Cover the whole of the exposed weft with buttonhole stitching or over and over stitching.

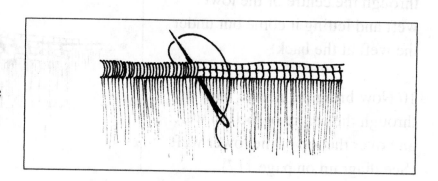

The marteau can be finished off by one of three methods:

1 By making a loop at each end, buttonholing over six strands of thread.

2 By sewing it to a postiche comb.

3 By sewing it to a postiche clip.

Before stitching it to the clip or comb, the weft must be pressed.

The double loop cluster

This section explains the making of a piece of postiche with a loop at each end.

Equipment needed

Weaving sticks and clamps

Drawing brushes

Precurled hair or the equipment for curling hair (see lesson five)

Jockey

Pinching irons

Tissue paper

Scissors

Needle

Thread to match the hair colour

Winding machine

Tail cord

This piece of postiche is designed to be added as a group of curls. For this reason we use short, precurled hair when making the double loop cluster.

Where would a double loop cluster be used?

1 On the crown, to give the appearance of long hair taken up into a chignon.

2 At the nape, either to cover up short nape hair or to give the appearance of a nape chignon.

3 Where the client's hair has receded slightly and the required style has a short curly fringe.

4 From the crown to the nape, long ways, to give the effect of cascading curls down the back.

Method

1 Check that the hair to be used is curled, permanently, to the requirements of the workroom order form.
If it is not, then this must be carried out before any weaving can be done.

2 Set up the weaving frame, using three lengths of weaving silk.

3 Place the hair to be woven, into the drawing brushes, the roots protruding.

4 Wind 20cms of clear weaving silk onto the left hand stick.

5 The first weaving to be done is two string fly weft, therefore the

....must be released slightly.

6 Start with a starting knot.

7 5cms of very fine, two string fly weft is woven.

8 Tighten up the bottom silk.

9 Without leaving a gap, continue weaving in once in weaving.
The amount of weaving depends upon the length of the finished piece.
This usually ranges between 30cms and 50cms.

10 Do not finish the once in weaving with a finishing knot.

11 After the once in weaving has been completed, a further 5cms of two string fly weft is woven. It does not help at this time to loosen the bottom silk as this may release the final few once in weaving movements.

12 Finish with a finishing knot for two string fly weft.

13 Press the weaving with heated pinching irons over tissue paper.

14 The weft is now cut down from the sticks.
NB There must be at least 20cms of clear silk at each end of the weft to allow the weft to slide along the silks whilst turning.

Sewing the double loop cluster

Method

1 Set up the winding machine.
Can you recall the other name for the winding machine?

....

Use tail cord to match the hair used for the weaving.

2 Thread a needle with thread to match the hair colour.

3 Find the centre of the weaving.

4 Stitch this point about 25cms up the tail cord.

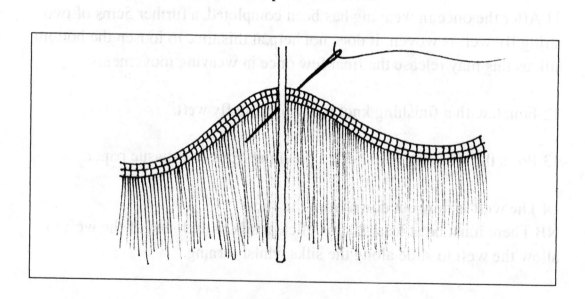

5 Sew one side of the weaving as you would for a one stem switch.

Allow the weft to spiral upwards on the cord.

Sew each turn.
The weft fits close to the tail cord, making a firm stem.

When the flyweft has been reached, cover approximately 5cms of silk with sewing thread.

Cut off and form a loop by stitching the tail cord to itself firmly.

Tie this loop back to the turning machine.

Wind the flyweft around, stitching securely.

Finally, make a silk cap by running sewing silk round.

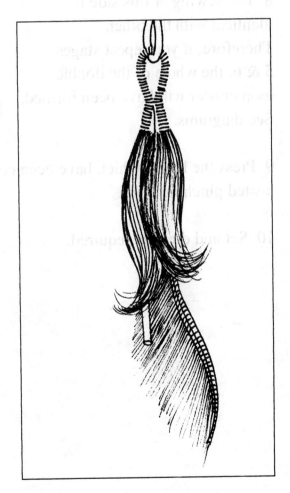

6 Remove the loop from the
turning machine.
You have now completed one half
of your double loop cluster.

7 Turn the weft the other way up
and begin again by sewing the half
way point to the tail cord.

8 The sewing of this side is
identical with the other.
Therefore, if you repeat stages
5 & 6, the whole of the double
loop cluster will have been formed.
See diagrams.

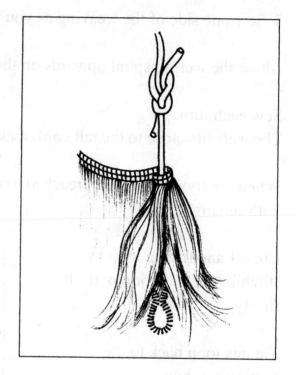

9 Press the loops, which have been covered with tissue paper, between
heated pinching irons.

10 Set and dress as required.

Weft wigs

Full wigs, made from weft, are the topic of this section.
They can be made from human hair or artificial hair.

Equipment required

Workroom order form

Weaving sticks and clamps

Weaving silk

Hair to be woven

Jockey

Pinching irons

Needle

Thread to match hair colour

Net

Malleable block

T pins

Postiche made from weft

Weft made wigs

The making of weft wigs by hand is a rare occurrence these days.

There are several reasons for this.

1 They are very heavy in appearance. This makes them easy to spot.

2 A natural appearance is hard to achieve.

3 Limited number of styles.

Method

1 Refer to the workroom order form.

2 Make a base similar to a cap. This can be made from stiff foundation net or a stretchy net. It should be made to hug the scalp.

3 Set up the weaving frame.

4 Place the hair into the drawing brushes.

5 Measure the outer perimeter and weave that amount in extremely fine fly weft. Remember to begin with a starting knot.

6 Next, weave between 20 and 25 metres of once in weaving.

7 Finish with a finishing knot.

8 Press the weaving, after covering with tissue paper, with heated pressing irons.

9 Cut the weft down from the silks and tie a knot at each end of the weaving.

Sewing the weft to the mount

1 Fix the net foundation to a malleable block, using T pins.

2 Thread a needle with silk to match the hair colour.

3 Start at the centre back and sew the starting knot, that is the flyweft, at the extreme edge. This is the only weft made postiche where the flyweft is stitched first.

4 The weft is now sewn to the base by winding it around and around. Each circuit of the head should be approximately 1cm ahead of the previous one. Stitch frequently as the movements progress.

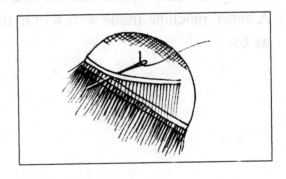

5 The final circle should have a diameter of 1 cm.

6 Set and dress as required.

Improvement

Occasionally, the wig can have the centre of the 1cm circle on the crown of the head knotted.

This is an attempt to disguise the wig.

Unfortunately it often just stands away from the rest of the hair.

Styles for weft wigs are mostly limited to those that fall towards the hairline from a central point on the crown.

If a parting is to be included in a weft made wig, this must be made before stitching the weft onto the base.

An area is then marked out onto the base, the size equal to the parting.

The weft is sewn from one side of the markings around the head to the other side.

Not very successful!

In the 'sixties a machine-made wig was introduced in this form.

The fact that the weft was made by a machine and the subsequent sewing was by machine, meant that the cost was cut quite dramatically.

A short, machine-made weft wig in the mid 'sixties could cost as little as £5.

Torsades

This section deals with a piece of weft made postiche rarely seen today.
I include it because I feel it is going to make a comeback.

Equipment required

Weaving sticks and clamps

Weaving silk

Hair to be woven

Jockey

Pinching irons

Needle

Thread to match hair colour

Net

Turning machine

The Torsade

What is a torsade?

It is a piece of postiche with curls at each end.

How is it made?

There are three methods of making a torsade.

1 Using four marteaux

2 Using two, one stem switches.

3 Using one, two stem switch and a length of short, curly weft.

Using four marteaux

1 Make four marteaux of equal size, but do not finish off with loops, clips or combs.

2 Sew together, along the top edge.

3 Take one of the marteau from the left, over to the right.

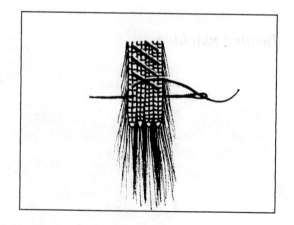

4 Take one marteau from the right, over to the left.

5 This is designed to cover the join.

Using two, one stem switches

1 Make two switches, each of one stem.

2 Take a loop in each hand.

3 Hold them about 8cms in from the points of the hair.

5 Coil the hair together, leaving the curly ends free.

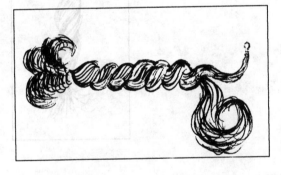

4 Stitch one loop to the hair.

6 Sew the other loop to the hair at the other end.

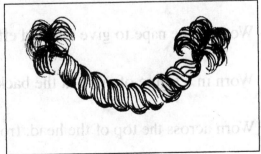

Using one, two-stem switch and a length of short, curly hair

1 Make up a two-stem switch.

2 Weave approximately 15 cms of fine, once in weaving using short, curly hair.

3 Coil the hair, allowing the curly ends to fly free.

4 Sew to secure.

5 Next, stitch the short curly weft around the base of the loop of the two stem switch.

Uses of the torsade

Worn at the nape to give a rolled effect, with curls over the ears.

Worn in a figure of eight at the back of the head.

Worn across the top of the head, from ear to ear, almost as a head band.

KEEPING THE VISION ALIVE

The Story of Barnardo's 1905-2005

WINSTON FLETCHER

This book is a testament to what has been achieved over the last hundred years to fulfil Thomas Barnardo's vision. I am delighted that Barnardo's is continuing its valuable work to help the UK's most vulnerable children and young people.

Her Majesty The Queen
Patron, Barnardo's

As Barnardo's President I have had the privilege of witnessing first hand how the charity helps vulnerable children across the UK to transform their lives. My work with Barnardo's has also given me an insight into how one man's dedication and vision more than a hundred years ago has shaped the charity and made it what it is today.

Keeping The Vision Alive, launched to commemorate the centenary of Dr Barnardo's death, explores the breadth of his legacy. It describes in detail the charity's humble beginnings – as Dr Barnardo wandered the slums of London's East End with cake in his pockets looking for homeless children to feed – right through to Barnardo's ground-breaking work in Britain today.

With such a wealth of history spanning three centuries, this book tells the inspirational story of Barnardo's throughout the ages, exploring how the charity has changed and adapted with the times.

From the orphanages of Victorian times to the charity's current work with children abused through the internet, Barnardo's has always believed that the most vulnerable and disadvantaged children deserve the best start in life and the chance of a better future. That was Dr Barnardo's vision all those years ago, and it remains the same today.

Barnardo's continued work with more than 100,000 disadvantaged children across the UK is keeping Dr Barnardo's vision alive. I wish Barnardo's every success with this vital work in its centenary year and beyond.

Cherie Booth QC

Dedicated to all Barnardo's staff and volunteers who have tirelessly helped thousands of disadvantaged and vulnerable children during the last century.

Contents

The Third Sector

A good society depends not on the state but on its citizens, acting on motives of various kinds, some selfish, others unselfish, some narrow and material, others inspired by love of man and love of God. The happiness or unhappiness of the society in which we live depends upon ourselves as citizens, not on the instrument of political power which we call the state.

Lord Beveridge (1942)

Today, a century after the death of its founder, Barnardo's is one of the UK's – indeed one of the world's – great charities. The charity Dr Thomas Barnardo founded is his paramount legacy, and this book celebrates that legacy. However the charitable work he carried out 100 years ago is very different from the work Barnardo's carries out today.

Barnardo's now directly helps more than 100,000 disadvantaged and vulnerable children each year, more than ten times as many as Tom Barnardo was able to help a century ago. Barnardo's now runs over 360 charitable projects nationwide. These projects help children and their families in a host of different ways. Not one of them, however, is an orphanage. Barnardo's stopped running orphanages, the work for which it was once so famous, more than 20 years ago. To understand how and why this radical change in Barnardo's work has come about, and to put Barnardo's historic and present achievements in perspective, we need first to explore the nature of charities today and their present role in society, and then move on to consider the changes in childcare which have occurred, many of them initiated by Lord Beveridge's vision, in the century since Tom Barnardo died.

Nowadays charities are often called the 'Third Sector', to distinguish them from the private and public sectors – highlighting the fact that they are motivated neither by profit nor by state-controlled public service: they sing from their own, distinctive song sheets. Like all Britain's leading charities, Barnardo's is a large

Above: An artist's impression of Dr Barnardo with destitute children.

Main picture: In June 2003, Her Majesty The Queen invited 200 Barnardo's children, among hundreds of others, to a picnic tea party at Buckingham Palace, celebrating the 50th anniversary of her coronation.

operation. Barnardo's annual revenue is approaching £200 million, while the entire charity sector exceeds £26 billion a year – almost 5% of Britain's gross domestic product. Despite its size, charity income grew by no less than 92% in the ten years 1993-2003, and it continues to outpace the economy, capturing an increasing share of the GDP almost every year. The sector employs around 600,000 people full time, more than the entire post and telecommunications industry. In addition, millions of part-time unpaid volunteers go out of their way to lend a generous hand. Barnardo's alone is helped by some 250,000 volunteers each year – working in shops, shaking boxes, collecting door-to-door, organising fêtes and musical events, making tea and doing a myriad other truly helpful things for no financial reward whatsoever. You can add to these the thousands of individual trustees, also unpaid, who guide and are legally responsible for the operations of Britain's charities. All of these people give of their time, effort and commitment for no other reason than that they like to. They understand perfectly Lord Beveridge's words:

> *A good society depends . . . on its citizens, acting on motives of various kinds, some selfish, others unselfish, some narrow and material, others inspired by love of man and love of God.*

For many young people the 'Third Sector' is now a particularly desirable area in which to work. It is much admired, even though it is often suspected of amateurish inefficiency. Every day, throughout the world, charities like Barnardo's improve the lives of millions of people, young and old. Charities are as international as the globe itself and as local as the tiniest hamlet. Charities support the arts, defend the environment and protect endangered species. They are constantly in the news, associated with famous stars who, like the helpers, give freely of their time and commitment. Elton John raises tens of millions to fight AIDS; Comic Relief's Red Nose Day dominates our television screens every other year and achieves both massive audience ratings and massive fundraising success; Donna Karan designs and markets T-shirts for the Twin Towers fund; Anya Hindmarch sells handbags for The Lavender Trust cancer charity; Sting protects the world's rainforests and Bill Gates has set up the largest charitable foundation the world has ever seen. In a largely secular world, outstanding charitable generosity is one of the few ways to be unequivocally respected in life, and remembered with honour in death. Charities are bejewelled with glamorous balls and dinners, and are one of the most consistently reliable sources of public honours – yet they are still stereotyped as the haunt of sandalled weirdos: kindly but unworldly do-gooders working for peanuts.

to good works, and you would (probably) reduce your time in purgatory: quite an incentive. With the Reformation and the demise of the sale of indulgences, Henry VIII in his Beggars' Act of 1536 permitted church elders to visit every local household and collect alms in official boxes. Given Henry VIII's less than charitable personal reputation, the pressure to donate would have been formidable. His Beggars' Act was just one of history's many attempts to regulate charity and reduce mendicancy: the beneficiaries were to be 'poor, needy, sick and indigent persons', and some of the alms were to be used to set the 'sturdy poor' to work.

Another historic truth about charity is that the poor are usually – within the limits of their capability and resources – the most generous donors. The Greek *epidoseis* were small gifts from the masses, while the story of the 'widow's mite', carried from Jewish tradition into St Mark's Gospel, epitomises the same truth. Having seen the widow donate two coins, worth one sixty-fourth of a daily wage, Jesus declared she had given more than anyone else, because she had given all she had. A study of sixteenth-century France shows food was given

Her Majesty The Queen presents to each of 76 women and 76 men (corresponding to her age in accordance with the tradition) two bags of Maundy Money, at Canterbury Cathedral in 2002.

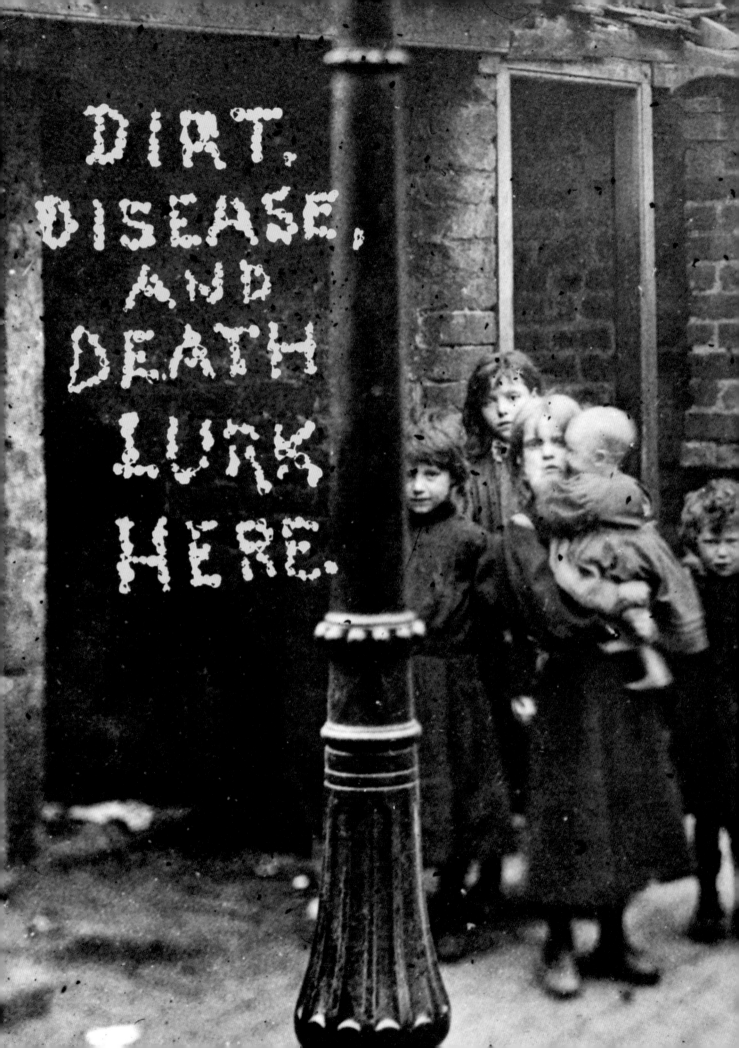

The Happiest Days of Your Life?

Barnardo's. The very name resonates. There is no other large charity in Britain named after its founder, and precious few smaller ones. People with a special interest may be acquainted with the names of some other founders of great charities. Not one of them has anywhere near the same wide level of public recognition as Dr Barnardo. This is doubly remarkable when you realise he died in 1905, a full century ago. Today the great majority of the British public know Dr Barnardo's name, and have at least a glimmering of what the charity he founded does. That many of the public believe Barnardo's still runs orphanages – which it stopped doing a couple of decades ago – is a backhanded compliment to the immense skill with which Barnardo publicised and marketed his work. If the fact that the charity still bears his name reflects, in some measure, Dr Barnardo's flamboyant egocentricity, it also – and much more importantly – reflects his incomparable success.

To appreciate his extraordinary achievements, and the inheritance he left, we need to explore how the economic and moral environment during the second half of the nineteenth century influenced attitudes to children, and look at how acutely things have altered since.

One of the many seismic changes wrought by the agrarian and industrial revolutions, and the consequent urbanisation of the population, was a profound transformation in the nature of childhood – a transformation with which we are still grappling today. The agrarian revolution, which drove workers off the farms, began early in the eighteenth century, and the start of the industrial revolution followed it half a century later. During the next hundred years urbanisation took hold. In 1800 the great majority of the population still lived in small rural communities. By the beginning of the twentieth century, when Dr Barnardo's work was at its peak, 80% of the population had moved into industrial towns, and one third of those were children. The population of London just about doubled between 1821 and 1851, and doubled again by the end of that century. For the poor, the overcrowding was insufferable.

Main picture: A London slum in the 1880s. The message was scratched on to the photographic plate by the photographer, appalled by what he had seen.

Above: A street urchin about the same time.

In the countryside, before urbanisation, most children grew up with their families and worked alongside their parents, boys in the fields and girls at home or in service. Scraping a living was so tough that the children's contribution to the family's earning power was vital. Indeed during the 16th century no fewer than five Parliamentary Acts were devoted to dealing with issues relating to children at work. Working long hours was the childhood norm. (Even kings were crowned and started work in their early teens.) Perhaps this was unexceptional when most people's life expectancy was less than forty years. Young human beings needed to get on with working and living, because their time on earth would be short.

All this meant children were perceived straightforwardly as young grown-ups, who hardly needed to be treated differently from adults except insofar as they were smaller and a little weaker. Over the next century, the industrial revolution tore this view of childhood up by the roots. Parents began to work in factories, for paltry wages and for agonisingly long hours, at jobs children could not easily perform. Nonetheless children continued to be employed alongside them, albeit for even more paltry wages. Nobody doubted children should be put to work. It was not until 1878 that protective legislation raised the earliest permitted age for employment in all factories and workshops to 10; it went up to 11 in 1891 and again to 12 in 1901.

Children whose parents were impoverished came under the jurisdiction of the 1834 Poor Law – which remained on the statute books, subject to constant and generally trivial amendment, for almost a century. The 1834 Act, always called the New Poor Law, created workhouses for the 'undeserving' poor and their children to live in, paid for by local taxes raised by local Poor Law unions (not to be confused with trades unions). The Victorians thought poverty to be shameful. The undeserving poor were those whom the powers-that-were believed to be poor of their own volition: they were called paupers, and were thought to be lazy, spendthrift and probably drunken. Even the extraordinarily generous philanthropist Andrew Carnegie, who was born into poverty and was an almost exact contemporary of Dr Barnardo, declared: 'Those worthy of assistance seldom require assistance. The really valuable men never do.' (But then Carnegie had pulled himself up by his bootstraps, became the richest man in the world, and doubtless felt all other poor children could and should do likewise.)

Lest there was any chance of paupers taking a liking to them, the newly created workhouses were deliberately designed to be unpleasant. In this, if in little else, they succeeded admirably. Most of the children in workhouses were there with one or both pauper parents, but about 20% of the children were parentless. These children

A scene of Victorian domestic bliss and moral rectitude, in extreme contrast to slum areas, probably not far away.

'The Outcast' by Richard Redgrave. The daughter with her illegitimate baby is turned out of the house by outraged, self-righteous father. This scene reflected social attitudes which Dr Barnardo fought to change.

had mostly been born in the workhouse and then lost their parents – usually a single mother who died in childbirth or not long thereafter. Mortality rates were horrendously high. As might be imagined, illnesses spread through the unsanitary workhouses like wildfire. And while the workhouses were provided for paupers, throughout the nineteenth century the state made little or no provision for the care of physically disabled children; this was simply left to their families, or to charities, or to fate.

The workhouses were reluctant, and too ill organised, to take in parentless beggar children from the streets. Such children tended to be particularly unruly and difficult to look after, and in workhouses they constituted yet a further cost to the local taxpayers. Moreover their legal status and their antecedents were all but impossible to verify. Local taxpayers might find themselves supporting migrant waifs and strays from other localities, which was not something they would relish. Nor did the waifs and strays seek accommodation in workhouses if they could avoid it. Workhouses were so terrible that in later Victorian times criminal children were flung into them as punishment. No sensible child wanted to live with the stigma of having grown up in a workhouse.

Needless to say premature death was not limited to workhouse inmates. Unsanitary living conditions, unhealthy diets and a lack of doctoring ensured that countless poor parents died young. Others deserted – or tried to desert – their children, who could be a crushing financial burden on them. Consequently the industrial revolution and urbanisation together resulted in an explosion of poverty-stricken, unemployed, often homeless and effectively parentless street children in all of Britain's larger towns, but especially in London. The exact number of such children is unknown, and could never have been known with any accuracy. They were a shifting population and their personal circumstances were constantly changing. But countless writers and commentators – from Dickens and Ruskin to Tom Barnardo himself – reported on their ubiquity. In a parliamentary speech in 1848 the great philanthropist Lord Shaftesbury put at a massive 30,000 the number of 'naked, filthy, lawless and deserted children roaming in London'. As the journalist John Hollingshead put it in 1861:

> . . . all the children who are not taken in by the ragged and other charity schools are always living in the streets: they eat in the streets, what little they get to eat, they play in the streets in all weather, and sometimes they have to sleep in the streets.

After visiting London in 1876 the eminent French historian Hippolyte Taine wrote that in the East End:

> Street boys abound, barefooted, dirty . . . on the stairs leading to the Thames they swarm, pale faced . . . In the alleys running into Oxford Street there were troops of pale children nestling on the muddy stairs.

Barnardo looked after some 60,000 poor and disabled children during the 40 years 1866–1905. In that last year of his life he had some 8,000 in his care. By then the total number of destitute children in London must greatly have exceeded the 30,000 estimated by Lord Shaftesbury about half a century earlier. The scale of child destitution in British industrial towns was prodigious.

Not surprisingly, a high proportion of these children turned to crime. During the nineteenth century juvenile delinquency burgeoned. As is clear from the social attitudes inherent in *Oliver Twist*, written in the late 1830s, the public then accepted juvenile crime to be omnipresent. That Fagin and Bill Sykes were able to run a fair-sized gang of young thieves manifestly surprised nobody. Such gangs were commonplace.

'The Nemesis of Neglect', *Punch,* 1888. Crime stalks the streets of the capital, in the period of Jack the Ripper, when fear pervaded the slums.

All this forced society to change its perceptions of childhood. Children could no longer be treated as little grown-ups, as they had been when they lived in the countryside. Many people saw the destitute youngsters as savages: some called them young Hottentots, or Kaffirs, or even less affectionately, social vermin. It was widely feared that so large an underclass of deprived and often criminal children could easily become – were already becoming – a threat to the stability of society. The public's fears were exacerbated, at the end of the century, by the unkempt, ill-behaved nature of many young soldiers recruited for the Boer War.

An increasing number of missionaries and anthropologists returned from Africa and the South Pacific during the nineteenth century, with tales of uncivilised primitive behaviour – the behaviour of human beings unfettered by education, by Christianity, or by British law and order. Maybe the 'savage' children would not automatically grow into hard-working, law-abiding, God-fearing adults? Heaven forbid. Left unchecked, they would surely grow up to be indolent, mutinous, lawless, heathen – a force for chaos and quite possibly revolution. Tom Barnardo himself published an article in 1879 entitled 'The Dangerous Classes'. Pointing to Nihilism in Russia and Socialism in Germany, he wrote: 'Every boy saved from the gutter is one dangerous man the less.' The missionary conception of savagery is masterfully captured in R. M. Ballantyne's *The Coral Island* (1857). This was itself the prototype for William Golding's classic, *Lord of the Flies* (1954), in which young Jack Merridew famously says: 'We've got to have rules and obey them. After all, we're not savages.' But as this novel so dramatically demonstrates, savage is just what children can easily become when left to their own devices. It was a view many Victorians shared. For the good of society, as well as for the good of their souls, destitute children needed to be civilised: they needed to be given work and brought to God. Helping destitute children was archetypical Victorian enlightened self-interest.

From early in the nineteenth century three ways to improve the lot of destitute children had already been identified, and it would be broadly true to say that these continued to be employed for well over a hundred years thereafter – though two of them passed into disuse in the second half of the twentieth century, when beliefs about the ways in which vulnerable children could and should be helped changed drastically.

The first of the three ways was taking children into institutional homes, often called orphanages though few of the children who lived in them were literally orphans. Most had a single parent who, for whatever reason, was unable to look after them. In the middle of the nineteenth century almost all of these homes were created and run by

One of hundreds of Thomas Barnardo's photos. This image brings to mind 'The Artful Dodger' in *Oliver Twist*.

Facing page, main picture:
Street urchin reminiscent of Charles Dickens' *Oliver Twist*.

Inset: Poster for a dramatisation of the novel.

Above: Lord Shaftesbury, philanthropist and founder of the Ragged School movement, was an early supporter of Dr Barnardo.

Below: Ragged School, Smithfield.

evangelical Christians. Probably the first was a Ragged School refuge, opened in 1852. (The Ragged Schools had been launched by the evangelical Lord Shaftesbury, in order to 'afford gratuitous instruction to children of the poor who have no other way of learning to read the word of God, and are deserving of the support of Christians of all denominations'.) In 1866 the same Lord Shaftesbury opened his first refuge on a ship, where children could more easily be isolated from harm. That year he claimed that he would soon be opening further refuge ships, which would completely solve the problem of urban child destitution. Lord Shaftesbury's achievements on behalf of poor children were manifold and remarkable, but in that claim he was sadly over-optimistic. Children are still being taken into local authority children's homes in Britain today.

The second way in which destitute children were helped to escape their plight was by being sent to the British colonies. Child emigration has had a long history. In the seventeenth century vagabond children were shipped to America, then itself a colony. Migration seemed to many of those working with neglected children to be a marvellous idea. It offered children a new life, in a country where young labour was needed and would be welcomed. In the nineteenth century emigration was pioneered by, once again, Lord Shaftesbury, through his Ragged School movement. In the late 1840s Shaftesbury asked for

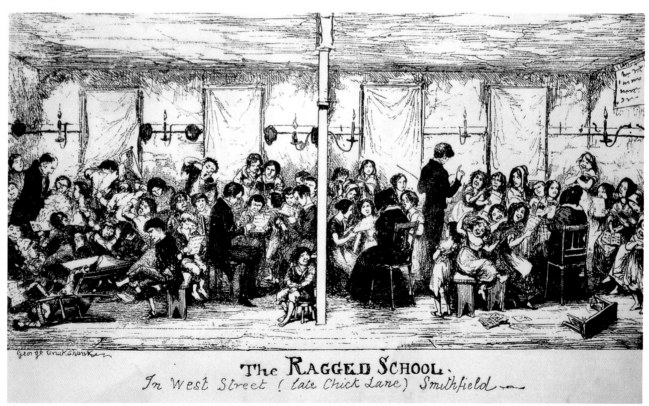

THE RAGGED SCHOOL.
In West Street (late Chick Lane) Smithfield

state aid to meet the cost of sending Ragged School pupils to work on sheep stations in Australia. As an experiment the government funded the emigration of 150 youngsters, but then refused to continue the funding. The Ragged Schools tried to continue on their own, but cash shortages led to the abandonment of this first scheme in the 1850s.

However, by then the government had passed the Poor Law Amendment Act which permitted Boards of Guardians to send workhouse children to Canada, and in the 1870s the main child emigration movement got under way. Emigration was seen to offer four major benefits. First, it moved destitute children out of overcrowded institutional homes in Britain, making room for new entrants – of whom there were always a plethora knocking on the doors. Second, it reduced the burden of expenditure for the homes, as once the travelling costs had been met the children earned their keep in their new country. In the 1880s it cost just £11 to kit out a child and meet all the costs of the journey. Third, it sent children to rural communities which were understandably believed to be far healthier, both physically and morally, than the decrepit slums in Britain from which they sprang. Fourth, it worked well for girls as well as boys. And there was one additional, incidental benefit: it was hoped that as they grew up the children, having been born in Britain, would help tie the colony more closely to the mother country. In 1879 the government itself started sending workhouse children to Canada, and this time the emigration continued for some five years, until a senior government inspector was sent over to review things. His report was largely unfavourable, particularly with regard to the long hours the children were forced to work. Consequently state emigration was suspended in 1885.

Nonetheless, many independent childcare institutions, including Dr Barnardo's from 1882 onwards, continued to send children overseas, believing their systems of supervision were sufficiently stringent to ensure the youngsters' protection. Following their lead, state emigration began yet again. It was a symptom of the country's desperate need to solve the problem of destitute children that emigration kept being tried and re-tried. Supporters of child emigration constantly referred to it as a 'spring transplanting', while opponents labelled it 'a life sentence of transportation into hard labour', and compared it to the penal despatch of criminals. Today the latter view tends to hold sway. Child emigration is widely viewed as heartless, and the records undeniably show that some children were subject to severe maltreatment: pitiless overwork, sexual assault and ferocious beatings. Other children, however, benefited hugely and loved their new lives. Both the state and private institutions continued to send poor children, on and off, to Canada (and later also to Australia) for nearly a century. The numbers sent peaked in the early decades of the twentieth century and began to dwindle thereafter, partly as a result of growing public hostility to the scheme. Child emigration ceased during the First World War but was restarted immediately afterwards when the government – deeply worried about the number and plight of war orphans – offered free passage plus £20 cash to charities for each child sent abroad. Child emigration finally ceased completely in 1967. By that time 150,000 poor children had been migrated from Britain.

Although residential homes and emigration are no longer tolerated as ways of helping homeless and vulnerable but otherwise healthy children, the third solution pioneered in the early nineteenth century is still widely accepted. Today it is called fostering; originally it was called, perhaps more descriptively, 'boarding out' – placing children in families which will look after them, provide surrogate parents and siblings, hopefully show them love and affection, and allow them to enjoy a home life that is as close as possible to that enjoyed by more happily endowed, and usually more affluent, children. Boarding out must not be confused with adoption. The biological parents of children who are adopted legally relinquish their offspring forever, and the children take their adoptive parents' surname. Children who are fostered, whether for weeks or for years, retain their separate identity and are never legally 'owned' by those who foster them.

Boarding out had been practised in England since the early 1800s, but was not common. It occurred much more extensively in Scotland, where it had been the practice for the previous two hundred years to place 'any beggar's bairn' with a respectable family. In Scotland boarding out had proved itself both efficient and satisfactory. In England it was popularised by Dr Barnardo himself, who spent a fair amount of time in Scotland. Starting in the 1880s, Barnardo quickly came to the conclusion that if it were properly managed, boarding out was not only advantageous for the child, it was also considerably cheaper to run. The cost of fostering a child was then around £13 a year, far less than the cost of maintaining a child in an institutional home. Moreover, as with emigration, children who were boarded out left room for new entrants to be educated and trained in his residential homes – prior to being themselves moved out into families, whether in the UK or abroad.

Boarding out rapidly took off. It is a great irony that to this day the Barnardo name is so inextricably linked with homes and orphanages, when the reality is that Dr Barnardo was himself a passionate believer in boarding out, and pretty well invented fostering in its modern form. Within five years of starting he was boarding out more than a thousand children annually. The homes to which he sent them had to be clean and sanitary, situated in districts far from factories and railway stations. The children and homes were regularly inspected by local committees set up for the purpose, usually based on the local church, and later by specially employed inspectors as well. Above all, the foster families had to be practising Christians – no child would be sent to an irreligious home, however worthy. To the

Barnardo's emigrants depart for Canada, 1909. The practice of emigration, which for its times had seemed enlightened and was followed by most children's charities, became increasingly out of favour, and ceased in later years.

fostering Christian family the income was an attractive financial bonus, even though it was emphasised to them that fostering must never be simply mercenary.

Today fostering has become the normal – almost the universal – mode of caring for children who cannot be brought up in their own troubled homes, with the rare exception of children who are seriously disabled. However, this switch away from institutional homes has not been without its opponents. As late as 1963, in an article in *The Observer*, Janet Hitchman – who had spent many years in care – wrote:

> *I am not madly in love with boarding out. Having been posted like a parcel all over Norfolk and known five different homes before I was eleven, I was thankful to sink into the anonymity of a children's home, where one was not expected to fulfil the motherhood urge of elderly spinsters, be an unpaid servant in a family, or a footstool to heaven for the righteous . . . a children's home is more under- standable to a small child than a home which is so like, but is not, his own home.*

Janet Hitchman pointed out that local authorities had a vested interest in switching children from homes to foster families. Fostering saved money, as it had always done. Today, keeping a child in a home costs a local authority about seven times as much as fostering. But Mrs Hitchman was swimming against the tide.

Today, the first aim of childcare is to keep the child with its own family, if at all possible, and to help its parents cope. This can be done in numerous ways, as we shall see. Very rarely will a healthy child be taken into managed residential care of any kind – and even then only for short periods. Nowadays it is almost unknown for able-bodied children to live most of their childhood, and be brought up, in a 'home'.

For a great majority of the British population life has changed immea-surably in the century since Dr Barnardo's death in 1905. There have been two pulverising World Wars; the introduction of the welfare state, and with it the National Heath Service; increased longevity and massively increased general affluence; a radical change in the role of women; a huge increase in divorce and a corresponding decline in the traditional family; a simultaneous, though unconnected, drop in both infant mortality and the birth rate; successive waves of immigration and a continuing fall in religious belief; together with more inventions and new technology than our grandparents could have dreamed of. These and many other changes have wrought tectonic changes on the

Lloyd George presents his People's Budget to the House of Commons in 1911. It followed his introduction of the Old Age Pension and National Insurance, precursors of Labour's Welfare State.

Labour Party election posters of 1950 promoting the benefits of the government's social legislation.

day-to-day lives of most Britons. The lives of children have also changed. But the lives of very poor and vulnerable children have changed far less than most.

Perhaps unsurprisingly, little of significance changed in the world of childcare between 1905 and the Second World War. The 1914-18 War began less than a decade after Dr Barnardo's death; it was followed by a relatively brief economic boom, and then the industrial strife of the 1926 General Strike, the great global stock market crashes of 1929 and the ensuing Great Depression of the 1930s, when there were more than 2 million unemployed in Britain. Society was badly awry and could hardly cope with its own problems, let alone those of disadvantaged young children. Moreover, during the 1930s, for the first time, large numbers of middle-class children found themselves in seriously impoverished circumstances: a new quandary to be coped with. It was not until the wartime Beveridge Report, which enshrined the thinking on which the 1945-51 Labour Government built the welfare state, that people began to look afresh at how society could ameliorate the lives of the very poor and vulnerable, and their children.

Admittedly, the 1834 Poor Law had been superseded by a 1930 Act which renamed Poor Law relief as 'public assistance' – an important emblematic modification. However, it was the 1948 National Assistance Act which really consolidated the change. The 1948

Planning for a better world. Sir William (later Lord) Beveridge, in 1942, at the height of the War, presents his blueprint for the Welfare State.

National Assistance Act charged local authorities with taking responsibility for most classes of vulnerable people in society. Social services were to be organised, administered and delivered locally, and individually, by local authorities and other statutory local agencies. Professional social service, as it has evolved in the last half-century, is deeply rooted in this post-war decentralised and individualised perspective.

At the core of Lord Beveridge's proposals was the extension of the national insurance scheme. Beveridge envisaged that almost everyone would pay national insurance contributions, and these would entitle them to flat-rate benefits which would protect them against real poverty during unemployment, sickness, old age and other contingencies. It was to be the end of all poverty! The impoverished would receive enough to live on, albeit little more than that. To be viable

Beveridge's system depended on almost full employment, and on the continuation of 'standard' family structures. In the event, a growing number of people found themselves outside the national insurance scheme, mostly as a result of long-term unemployment, lone parenthood, poor health or disability – groups for which Beveridge had made no special provision. It was not until the 1970s, for example, that benefits were introduced to meet the specific costs arising from disability.

After Beveridge, as the War ground to a halt in 1945, the Government set up a committee, chaired by Dame Myra Curtis, to consider the plight of the children who had been made homeless, and sometimes parentless, during the preceding six-year conflict. This was a sizeable national problem: there were an estimated 125,000 such children 'deprived of a normal home life'. In 1946 the committee published its recommendations, known as the Curtis Report, which changed forever the ways in which the care of dispossessed children was approached in Britain. First and foremost, Curtis recommended adoption as the very best option for children without parents or a satisfactory home. If adoption was not possible, then fostering was the second-best option. Only those children who could neither be adopted nor fostered should be placed in an institutional home, and – the Report urged – such homes should always be small, housing 12 children at the very most, for both sexes, and as close as possible to where the children's family lived. For a charity then called Dr Barnardo's Homes, which owned many large residences in the rural south east, the Curtis Report took some digesting – despite the fact that it had co-operated fully with the Curtis committee, and had long accepted the benefits of fostering.

Following hard upon the Curtis Report, the 1948 Children Act incorporated many of its proposals. Above all, the Act recognised that the care of children was the nation's responsibility, and introduced a legislative framework to protect the needs of all children whose parents could not, or would not, look after them. It established that every local authority must have a separate children's committee, served by a separate children's department.

The underlying philosophy of the Curtis Report was taken still further by the 1963 Children and Young Persons Act. Rather than take children into homes, local authority children's departments were required to give advice, support and, if necessary, financial assistance to families in difficulties. Indeed, such was the growing antipathy towards homes, the Act gave local authorities specific powers to stop children being taken into them.

The new children's departments were just one of numerous social care departments that legislation required local authorities to provide,

Myra Curtis, Principal of Newnham College, Cambridge, headed the committee which investigated the plight of Britain's 'forgotten children', culminating in the ground-breaking Curtis Report.

Barnardo's *Parenting Matters* programme, covers such topics as positive discipline, coping with problems experienced by most parents at some time or another.

Above: The programme recognises the cultural differences faced by ethnic minorities.

Facing page: The charity's centre at Fulford Family Centre, Bristol.

so that the cost of the welfare services escalated relentlessly. Between 1949-50 and 1992-93 real expenditure on social security, at constant prices, increased by over 700%, and went from 4.7% to 12.3% of the gross domestic product, which was itself growing steadily. This seemingly inexorable surge in the cost of welfare services was one of the Thatcher Government's greatest causes for concern in the 1980s – and became a cause of concern for all political parties in the 1990s. Throughout this period governments set up committees to report on the problems: the Seebohm Report (1968), the Barclay Report (1982) and the Griffiths Report on Community Care (1986) all brought fresh perspectives to the issues, but failed to find ways to curb the costs.

One reason for the cost explosion was that different local government departments had to deal with different social problems. This was a direct consequence of the 1948 National Assistance Act, and led to boundary wars between the departments, as well as much wasteful duplication of resources. People from different departments often visited the same problem families, one after the other. Following Seebohm, the 1970 Local Authority Social Services Act established that each authority should unite its various social services in a single, expanded operation. This seemingly sensible change misfired badly. Social work was a new profession, and many individual social workers had neither the experience nor the training to deal with a wide variety of family problems. The reputation of social workers and social work

foundered – a problem that lingers in some quarters to this day. In the 1970s and 1980s there was much discussion of whether social work was a viable profession at all. The 1982 Barclay Committee was riven with internal fractures – which reflected the unhappy state of social work itself at that time – and its findings hardly moved matters forward. However the Griffiths Report, which was followed by the 1989 Children Act, separated children's and adult social services without setting up a multiplicity of different local authority departments, and laid the foundations for the structure of social services which survived almost until the present day. However the killing of little Victoria Climbié in 2000 highlighted severe shortcomings in the organisation of statutory childcare, which the newest Children Act has been designed to address.

Ever since the 1948 National Assistance Act local authorities have found it difficult to recruit sufficient social workers, of a high enough standard, to do all the work with which legislation has charged them (particularly within their often straightened budgets). When they are unable to cope themselves, local authorities often meet their obligations by turning to charities and working closely with them. Well before 1948, the welfare charities, including Barnardo's as would be expected, had long experience of helping vulnerable people, whether they be young or old, abused or homeless, permanently disabled or temporarily afflicted. Charities had the staff, the premises, and the expertise: they were ready, willing and able to help.

Moreover, for many needy and disadvantaged people the reputation of the leading charities has always been more appealing, more kindly and more humane, than the reputation of local authorities. Town halls and local government offices are intimidating ports of call for vulnerable people. They feel more comfortable being helped by friendly charity workers than, as they see it, by impersonal government employees. And indeed, local authorities are quite often forced to take tough decisions, which rebound badly on those who are relying on them – and rebound equally badly on local authorities' reputations. Furthermore some, though by no means all, very good social workers prefer to work for charities rather than for government organisations. (Though it must be emphasised that there is a great deal of employment interchange between the charities and the local authorities. Many if not most social workers nowadays work for both types of employer during the course of their career.) For all these reasons town halls and charities have become increasingly entwined.

But while local authority social services were organising, re-organising and re-re-organising themselves and struggling to cope during the latter part of the twentieth century, four other, perhaps equally fundamental, forces were at work in the field of childcare:

- *A growing and implacable hostility towards institutional homes.*
- *A boom in both divorce and in one-parent families.*
- *A sizeable influx of young immigrants, and – inconceivable though it may seem –*
- *A significant growth in child poverty.*

From the 1948 Children Act onwards, social workers began seriously to question the acceptability of ever bringing up children in institutional homes. Part of their hostility may have been political: children's homes were (and are) associated in the public mind with workhouses and with an implicit condemnation of 'unworthy' poor people. Most of their criticisms, however, were practical rather than political, and well founded. Despite the valiant defence put forward by Janet Hitchman and others, and despite the immense and kindly efforts made by the best of those in charge of children's homes – some of whom were veritably saintly – many homes were harsh institutions, devoid of love or even affection. Children were not infrequently abused, sexually or otherwise – often sexually and otherwise. In an increasingly enlightened and socially conscious society this became utterly unacceptable. Olive Stephenson, a leading social worker who became a professor of social studies, wrote in 1995 of her experience in the 1950s:

> *I find myself remembering the negative effects of institutional life for thousands of people . . . we needed to close as many residential nurseries as possible, being utterly convinced of the damage to young children of institutional processes.*

Simultaneously, the shake-up in the traditional family caused by explosions in the number of divorces and of one-parent families was taking hold. Divorce became ten times more common after the Second World War. Today about 150,000 children live through parental divorces each year; more than 1,250,000 children now live in step-homes – one in ten of all children. And twice as many children, well over 2,500,000, now live in single-parent families. In total over one-third of all children do not live with both biological parents. A disproportionate number of these children need special help and care during their childhood.

To add to these problems there has been a boom in immigration, particularly in recent years. The problems of immigrants are far from new, and it is much to Dr Barnardo's credit that he himself recognised no racial barriers: from the start he treated children of all ethnic origins equally. At the time of his death, when immigration was comparatively low, there were over 400 children from Asia, Africa, the

USA, the West Indies and elsewhere in Barnardo's homes. But at that time the total number of immigrants coming to live in Britain was relatively tiny. Though the numbers have recently fallen, in the first years of the twenty-first century around 120,000 people annually were being granted settlement here, more than twice as many as a decade ago. Many immigrants live in Britain for years before being given settlement, during which period their lives, and the lives of their children, are especially precarious. Almost inevitably such families often need help.

For these and other reasons, towards the end of the twentieth century child poverty in Britain mushroomed. Most of the public are astonished when they learn that, according to official government data, over 12 million people today live in poverty, of whom nearly one quarter are children. People argue about the official definition of poverty – an annual income below 60% of the country's median income – but the argument is largely irrelevant. Poverty remains the largest single threat to any child's future. Children born into poverty

Children born into poverty are more likely to lack opportunities and have reduced hopes and aspirations.

lack opportunities and have reduced hopes and aspirations, both for themselves and for their own children. They are more likely than others to end up homeless, to have problems with drugs and alcohol, and both to commit crimes and themselves to be the victims of crimes. In certain grim regions of the country, just as in Victorian times, levels of child poverty are well above the national average. Child poverty rises to 48% in inner London, and there are some electoral wards in Britain where the figure exceeds 90%.

The Labour government which came to power in 1997 pledged itself to eliminate child poverty within 20 years. The administration significantly increased expenditure on the social services, and nowhere has this been more apparent than in the welfare charities and voluntary organisations. As the twentieth century ended and the twenty-first century began the social welfare charities saw their income and their work from government agencies increase appreciably. Nonetheless, 100 years after Dr Barnardo's death child poverty remains deeply ingrained in British society – and poor children still need all the help they can be given.

Naturally, poverty is not the only unkind fate to befall children. Affluent children, too, abuse drugs and alcohol; they too are abused physically and sexually by adults, and are lured into prostitution. Children from all social strata are born – or can become – disabled physically, psychologically and behaviourally. Local authorities cannot cope with all these problems alone, any more than the government agencies could cope with the child destitution that was rife when Thomas Barnardo began his charity work. To minimise the pain and suffering which poverty, abuse, disability and other disadvantages still cause hundreds of thousands of British children each year, the authorities need to work hand-in-hand with the children's charities. Barnardo's is at the forefront of this work – as it has been since its founder began his philanthropic work some 140 years ago.

The social pressures on young people remain as great a challenge to our society as ever.

Thomas John Barnardo

Do I contradict myself?
Well then I contradict myself,
(I am large, I contain multitudes)

Walt Whitman

The fine American poet Walt Whitman, a contemporary of Dr Barnardo, well knew that his lines encapsulate a truth about all human beings: we all contradict ourselves from time to time. But of few people can the lines have been truer than of Tom Barnardo himself.

Thomas John Barnardo was blessed with an extraordinary profusion of talents and abilities. Directly or indirectly, he influenced many aspects of childcare during the last 100 years. Yet he was a man with an abundance of inconsistencies. He devoted his life to serving others with immense kindness and generosity, but was fearsomely egocentric; he built one of the greatest charities in Britain but was quick to anger and attacked his enemies unremittingly; he was fiercely energetic and driven, but frequently took to his bed with unidentified ailments – perhaps stress-related, perhaps even depressive; he was well aware of how much he depended on his staff, but constantly browbeat and bullied them. From an early age he was a fervent Christian evangelist, but it seems quite likely his distant paternal ancestry was Jewish; he lived and worked among the very poorest and ill-clad classes of society, but was something of a dandy; he was an incomparable fundraiser, and for most of his life he was a member of the Plymouth Brethren, one of whose tenets was 'owe no man anything' – but when he died his charity was £249,000 in debt; he waged war against the pernicious effects of alcohol, but in his later years was not averse to a tipple at bedtime; though he could not have condoned gambling he took a party of children to the Epsom Derby every year; he abhorred the theatre and averred it was responsible for much individual and public evil, but loved being a showman and was a fabulous impresario. Most remarkable of all, he was known everywhere, and is known to this day, as

Above: Barnardo with two of his sons, c. 1888.

Main picture: Tom Barnardo at his desk.

Tom Barnardo's mother Abigail and his father John Michaelis.

Doctor Barnardo, but – largely because his charity work took over his life in his early twenties – he never fully qualified as a doctor of medicine.

Tom Barnardo's father John Michaelis married Abigail, Tom's mother, in the German Church in London on 23 June 1837. Abigail was the sister of John Michaelis' first wife Elizabeth, who had died giving birth to her seventh child. John and Abigail both lived in Dublin, and they probably married in London because at that time it was not legal in Britain for a man to marry two sisters. However John was a Prussian citizen and was able to sidestep British law by re-marrying in the German church.

Thomas John was the fifth child of John Michaelis' second marriage, his father's twelfth offspring. He was born on 4 July 1845, and it was a difficult birth. His mother was too ill to nurse him, and he was put in the care of a wet nurse in Dublin. Thomas John's earliest days were spent in the care of the nurse and of his eldest half-sister Sophie, who doted on him. He was a plain, sickly and difficult child, constantly outshone by his enchanting younger brother Henry Lionel. Henry Lionel had fair curly hair and a sweet singing voice, and was frequently shown off to admiring visitors. Left in his bedroom upstairs, Thomas grew strong-willed and fractious, not to say petulant. He never grew taller than 5 foot 3 inches, always had poor eyesight, went deaf in his 50s and throughout his life was subject to long bouts of debilitating illness.

His father was a furrier, and had been fairly wealthy before Tom was born, but lost a good deal of money on the stock market at about the time of his birth – a fact that was to be of considerable significance in the child's later life. There is no record of Tom's educational achievements, but he wrote that the Principal of his school, the Reverend William Dundas, was 'the most cruel man as well as the most mendacious that I have ever in all my life seen! He seemed to take a savage delight in beating his boys.' Barnardo later ascribed his violent detestation of any form of child cruelty to these long remembered early experiences. The other major formative experience of his youth was the religious revival that swept through Ireland in 1859. At that time Tom was only 14, but Christian fervour took strong hold with his mother and siblings, though not with his father. Tom himself – having previously insisted that he was an agnostic – was 'converted' in 1862, when he was 17.

Tom Barnardo always referred to his religious conversion as the most momentous event in his life, after which his life was never the same again. Undeniably this was so. He soon left the established Church of Ireland and joined the Plymouth Brethren. This was another defining moment. The Brethren were Biblical fundamentalists, preoccupied with the imminent second coming of Christ, which they were sure would precede the millennium. This gave many of them a powerful sense of urgency; they were convinced there would be no salvation for those lacking knowledge of, and acceptance of, the Gospel's truths. To them, and to Tom Barnardo, it was vitally important to save human beings' souls before it was too late.

In 1865 the evangelist orator Hudson Taylor, who had founded the China Inland Mission, visited Dublin. Promoting his mission, Taylor avowed that there were 'a million a month dying in China without knowing Christ'. Tom Barnardo found his first great cause. He was nearly 20, and he wanted action. Despite the fierce opposition of his father, who had not embraced Christianity with as much zeal as the rest of the family, Tom left for London in 1866 en route for China. In London he planned to become a doctor, so he could be of more help in China.

His father having refused to finance his venture, Tom found cheap lodgings in the East End of London. At that time London's East End was so squalid, unhealthy, stinking and crime-ridden, that few outsiders ever visited the area – let alone chose to live there. Barnardo had only been there a few months when an outbreak of cholera swept through the locality, killing over 3,000 people and leaving many stricken families destitute. He himself saw 16 people die in one day. Tom Barnardo was viscerally compassionate. Though his thoughts were still fixed on working in China, he visited and prayed with many of the sick and dying in their fever-stricken hovels. It was not until the following year that he registered as a medical student at the London Hospital on Whitechapel Road.

By now he was already beginning to undertake philanthropic work. Later he claimed his East End work with children began in 1866, and this has now been accepted as the birth date of the Barnardo's organisation. But with his eyes still set on China, the truth probably is that his first charity work in London was somewhat ad hoc, an instinctive response to the dreadful conditions around him. He had no long-term plan to make it his life's vocation, as he so passionately wanted to go to China. Nonetheless, by 1870 he was doing so much work in London's East End that both he and the China Inland Mission realised he could not just up sticks and leave. He advertised for someone to take over his work, but found nobody. He then dropped for good his plan to go to China. This removed the main incentive for his medical studies, and he ceased to attend the London Hospital long before completing them.

Meanwhile he had taken to being a preacher. In the late 1860s he started preaching in the festering streets of Stepney, enduring jeers,

A formal photographic portrait used on Tom Barnardo's visiting card.

39

rotten eggs, mouldy fruit, dollops of mud and slops thrown at him for his efforts. The meagre results he achieved did not deter Barnardo – either then or ever. Courage in the face of adversity was one of his abiding qualities. He also started to teach at one of Lord Shaftesbury's Ragged Schools for impoverished children, off the Mile End Road. His teaching abilities and his skill with children soon attracted the attention of the school committee. He was quickly made a superintendent, and promoted to the governing committee – but before long he began to quarrel with other committee members, and he resigned. This was a pattern of behaviour that was to recur throughout his life. A letter written to Hudson Taylor in 1869 by a member of the China Inland Mission in London reads:

> *While Thomas Barnardo is a very talented fellow he is so overbearing that it tries some of us a little.*

A couple of years earlier Barnardo had begun writing short stories. The first of them, 'The Eleventh Hour', was published in July 1867 in a weekly religious magazine called *The Revival*. As a youngster Barnardo had read widely, but after his conversion he ceased to read any book but the Bible, from which long quotations appear frequently

A pupil and, *below*, a pupil's report from one of Shaftesbury's Ragged Schools.

Nᵒ 11. Ebenezer Davis, aged 17 years, admitted Junʳ 15ᵗʰ 1856. Father in Lambeth Workhouse, a dissolute bad character. Has been away from his parents for several years. Used to work at a Fireworks factory but never had any regular employment. Imprisoned three times. Can neither read nor write, yet quick & intelligent. Quarrelsome, untruthful and insincere. August 27ᵗʰ 1856. Sailed for Canada in the "City of Hamilton". Baptized at Walton church, July 25ᵗʰ 1856 caused great anxiety the first few months he was in the Refuge, but he changed very greatly, he acquired better control over his temper, and seemed to feel his religious obligations. He left us with strong hopes that the good seed would bear fruit in him." Novʳ 9ᵗʰ 1856, arrived at Kingston. Being late in the season had much difficulty in finding employment

in his letters. As soon as he began to write graphic stories about the poverty and distress he saw around him his natural ability to convey life in the East End blossomed – and his career as a writer blossomed with it. He had real literary talent. Throughout his life he continued to write prolifically for any number of publications. He founded two successful magazines, *The Children's Treasury* and *Night and Day*, principally to publicise his charitable work and thus to raise money. At one time he edited both simultaneously, working long into the night to do so. Writing was his main source of personal revenue throughout his life, and in his later years earned him the considerable income of around £2,000 a year.

But in 1868, while he was still a medical student and was preaching and writing, he opened his Juvenile Mission, a home for needy and vulnerable children. This was his first major move into childcare. With the help of friends he rented two small adjoining houses in Stepney. In one house he put boys, in the other girls. Right from the start he kept boys and girls separate, though most homes did not. Tom Barnardo's home was utterly unlike a workhouse in that it was designed to be a pleasant, if strictly regimented, place to live. It was a place where children would be educated and taught a vocation; and parents (if they even existed) were not allowed to live there. Indeed living parents who consigned their children to Dr Barnardo's care were usually forced to relinquish all further rights to them, at least for a lengthy period. This was a *quid pro quo* for the free shelter, food, clothing and education he provided.

A few months after he opened his Juvenile Mission he published his first report – showing how aware he was of the need for publicity. The report makes clear that the motivation for his work with children was, as he put it, 'to prepare them for heaven'. Great though he was as a philanthropist, first and foremost he was always an evangelist. In the courtyard outside the two houses he began to hold open-air prayer services, as well as to officiate at baptisms and to persuade men who swore and drank to give up their wickedness and convert to Christianity.

About this time Barnardo encountered Jim Jarvis, the first truly destitute child he had ever met. This was one of his life's great epiphanies. He told the story countless times, and later insisted the encounter had occurred in 1866 – to justify his claim to have started his charity work in that year – but it seems more likely that the true date of the meeting with Jim was during the winter of 1869-70.

Barnardo's first rendition of the full story, which he polished and embroidered a little during its many retellings, appeared in 1872 in *The Christian* magazine under the title 'How it all happened'. In the story Barnardo met Jim Jarvis when he was teaching at the Ragged

Donkey Stable, the original building used by Barnardo as a Ragged School.

Jim Jarvis shows Dr Barnardo the waifs on the London streets. This picture was used to illustrate the Jim Jarvis story.

School. At the end of the school day Jim didn't want to go home ('I ain't got no mother'). He was sleeping out ('along o'the 'aymarket in one of them carts as is filled with 'ay . . . perhaps you'd let me lie 'ere near the fire all night? I won't do no 'arm, sir . . .'). Is it possible, Tom Barnardo wondered, whether 'in this great city there are others like this young boy'? 'Oh yes sir, lots, 'eaps of 'em! More 'n I could count!' Jim told him. Barnardo took Jim back to his room, fed and warmed him, and then asked him about his life. Jim's mother had died five years previously, since when he had stayed in workhouses, or slept rough, been thrashed and beaten up, and often had no food. Worse still, when Barnardo asked Jim if he had heard of Jesus, the boy replied, 'sinking his voice into whisper, "He's the Pope o' Rome".' That evening, as his writings show, Barnardo decided Jim had been a direct message to him, sent by God. He decided to commit himself to saving destitute children. Swiftly he realised that he could not compete with poverty and hunger. If he was to bring children to Christ, he must first relieve their poverty. And because the second advent was imminent, there was no time to lose.

Tom Barnardo had arrived in London inexperienced and penniless. Within five years his Juvenile Mission would be recognised as one of the largest and fastest growing in the East End. Within ten years he was collecting and handling, more or less single-handedly, donations of more than £25,000 a year. This considerable expansion could not have been achieved without the help of the network of nonconformist evangelists who supported him, both spiritually and financially. There were upper-class families like the Aberdeens, Kinnairds, Kintores, Pelhams and Waldegraves; and there were wealthy middle-class families, many of them bankers, like the Barclays, Bevans, Dennys and Tritons. They all knew each other, and they quickly spotted Tom Barnardo's remarkable gifts as a speaker, writer, fundraiser, teacher and philanthropist.

Of all the evangelical philanthropists, Lord Shaftesbury was unquestionably the leader – though this was a description he himself would have eschewed. Barnardo later came to see himself as Lord Shaftesbury's successor, but in truth his relationship with the statesman was somewhat ambiguous. Barnardo, for example, claimed that after a dinner at Lord Shaftesbury's home attended by 14 or 15 others, he told them the story of Jim Jarvis and then took them all to Billingsgate so they should see for themselves the 'lays' in which boys slept under tarpaulin. According to Barnardo, Shaftesbury whispered to him, 'All London shall know of this.' But Shaftesbury had spoken in Parliament about the 30,000 destitute children in London back in 1848. Nonetheless he was much impressed by Barnardo, and supported his early work – though, like many others in the years to come, he was concerned from the start about Barnardo's ability to manage his affairs wisely.

At this time Barnardo often made courageous night-time forays alone into London's nether world, dressed in his oldest clothes, lantern in hand and with cake in his pockets to give to the waifs he met. He brought back destitute lads 'whose poor wan faces and ill-nourished bodies betoken their previous histories'. By now Barnardo had moved into larger premises on Stepney Causeway. Life for the boys in his care was strictly regulated – a fact noted with approval by many visitors. Barnardo was a strong believer in the moral worth of hard work, both for himself and for his boys. Discipline was rigorous. The boys were taught various trades: there were brush-making, tailoring and shoemaking shops on the premises, and he set up the City Messenger Brigade, all of which earned good money for both the home and the boys. This vocational training was one of the major benefits of life in a Barnardo's home. There was also a schoolmaster responsible for the boys' education. Their religious tuition took place in the home as well, Barnardo being unwilling for them to go to churches or chapels where 'the truth of God might be hard to under-stand'. The fundamentals of this regime did not change for many decades to come, and it is easy to see why it came to be viewed as restrictive and restricting: it provided an over-institutionalised childhood.

City Messengers with their young inspector. Postcard, c.1872.

E. E. J. M.—Home for Working & Destitue Lads.

No. 11.—A GROUP OF CITY MESSENGERS WITH THEIR YOUNG INSPECTOR.

The Edinburgh Castle, the public house purchased with funds raised by Barnardo and converted to house his first mission.

Meanwhile, Barnardo's horizons were expanding beyond childcare. The destructive power of alcohol – the only earthly solace available to the poverty-stricken inhabitants of the East End – was gradually becoming a matter of great concern to the evangelists. They began to see the tavern as the greatest rival to the church. Barnardo began tabulating the causes which led to children coming into his care, and 85% of cases were the result of parental drinking. He started to campaign in favour of temperance. On one occasion when he entered a beer house, preaching and selling pamphlets, he was beaten up by drunken youths and had two ribs broken. He refused either to be deterred or to bring charges against his attackers: 'I began with the gospel and was determined not to end with the law,' he said – a decision which won him much local respect.

His evangelical zeal was matched by his entrepreneurial flair. Early in 1872 Barnardo raised the money to erect a mission tent outside a large local tavern called the Edinburgh Castle. The tent held over 2,000 people, and became hugely popular as – in addition to himself – Barnardo employed first-class preachers. Out of the blue that summer, the Edinburgh Castle came onto the market for £4,000. With characteristic bravado Barnardo decided to buy it. Calling it 'the Citadel of Satan' he launched a fundraising campaign. Quickly he

Barnardo's head offices at Barkingside today.

received the support of several wealthy backers. Increasingly confident, Barnardo bought Satan's Citadel before he had even raised the entire purchase price. It was touch and go, but by the day of completion he had the money, and £100 more besides. The audacity of this astonishing coup brought Barnardo his first taste of fame and public acclaim.

It also went to his head. In November 1872, when he was 27, he gave orders that in future he was to be known as Dr Barnardo, and from early 1873 onwards he was always referred to as 'Doctor'. Before long he was accused of using the title without the right to do so. Beleaguered, and over-anxious to defend himself, he responded with uncharacteristic folly. He claimed he had obtained an M.D. (by mail order) from the obscure University of Giessen in February 1872, and produced a letter purporting to prove it. Unhappily, though Barnardo had certainly been in contact with the University of Giessen, the letter granting him a doctorate proved to be bogus. However, after a period of study in Scotland, in 1876 he qualified in surgery and obstetrics at the Royal College of Surgeons in Edinburgh (and in 1879 he was elected a Fellow of this Royal College). Nonetheless he did not complete his medical studies and therefore never acquired all the qualifications necessary to practice as, and assume the title of, 'doctor'.

Lord Cairns, one of Tom Barnardo's
staunchest supporters.

'Carrots' and the barrel,
his 'home', in which he
eventually froze to death.

But the Edinburgh Castle was a massive success. Outside Barnardo hung a signboard which proclaimed 'No drunkard shall inherit the Kingdom of God'. He had the interior ambitiously redecorated 'with mirrors and bright paintings', and it sported a library, a smoking and reading room, and club rooms; cocoa, coffee, tea and other non-alcoholic drinks were sold in warm and comfortable surroundings. It made a profit right from the start. Above all, it provided a splendid mission hall, and Barnardo preached there every week. Over the following nine years he preached at least one thousand different sermons, each one neatly written out in his own hand. In addition to everything else he was doing, this was a formidable workload. Then, in the tenth year after its purchase, serious cracks occurred in the building's structure. Undaunted, Barnardo raised the money to demolish and completely rebuild it, enlarging it in the process. Amid much rejoicing the Lord Chancellor, Lord Cairns – who became one of Barnardo's staunchest supporters – presided at the re-opening ceremony in 1884. No fewer than 3,000 people could now be accommodated. Barnardo himself, however, became less involved with the Edinburgh Castle thereafter, leaving its running to others. Once again he was restlessly moving on.

In the early 1870s Barnardo had been much moved by the fate of a lad called John Somers, always known as 'Carrots' because of his red hair. Carrots had no father, and his mother had cast him adrift on the streets. One night he sought refuge in Barnardo's Stepney boys' home, but the home was full and he was turned away. Two nights later, at the age of 11, he froze to death while sleeping in a barrel in Borough Market. Carrots' tragic story, like that of Jim Jarvis, had a transforming impact on Tom Barnardo. He determined that no such thing should ever recur – concerned, it must be said, as much by Carrots' lack of religious knowledge at the time of his death as by the death itself. Barnardo announced that in future his policy would be 'No Destitute Boy Ever Refused Admission'. This bold and challenging promise, known as 'The Ever Open Door', caused constant financial and organisational strains over the years. But it was the principle on which Barnardo's homes were run forever thereafter. However the policy initially applied only to boys, not to girls, about which Barnardo was far from happy.

From the outset he had aimed to care for both sexes. Despite the obvious reputational risks for a bachelor, he had brought back street girls to his first female residence. The physical risks and hazards facing destitute girls were similar to those facing boys, but naturally even worse. Now he wanted to make the same uncompromising promise of shelter to destitute girls as he had made to boys. In the early 1870s an opportunity arose for him to solve the problem. He may even have seen it as baldly as that, given his temperament and his ambitions. He would get married.

Tom met Syrie Elmslie when he was invited to preach at a Ragged School she ran in Richmond, Surrey. About 18 months later their paths crossed again at the funeral of an evangelical minister. Tom proposed. Her relatively affluent family did not conceal their dismay at the prospect of such a marriage. Barnardo was by then 28, but had no profession, no settled home, no likely inheritance and no regular income – and he already had weighty responsibilities. Syrie at first turned down 'the little rascal', but he was as determined and persistent as ever. Before too long, despite her family's misgivings, Syrie accepted.

Barnardo blatantly used their wedding as an opportunity to publicise his wish to open a home for girls. He achieved his aim. As a wedding present a supporter gave the newly-weds a 15-year lease on Mossford Lodge in Ilford, to be used both as their own home and as a home for destitute girls. With 'the voluntary help of some Christian ladies', Tom and Syrie would 'train up a band of kitchen maids, dairy maids, laundry maids and cooks to meet the great demand everywhere for cleanly and instructed female servants'. To rescue girls on any scale would be another massive, self-imposed challenge. Barnardo was not deterred. Unfortunately, Syrie proved less adept at running homes than her workaholic husband. And girls proved less amenable than boys to living institutionally in a large home. It was not possible, Barnardo soon discovered, to bring up sixty motherless street girls under one roof and train them to be properly ladylike. One night he overheard the girls talking and was horrified by their 'vile conversation . . . by aggregating these girls I was propagating and intensifying evil.' Little more than a year after Mossford Lodge was opened, Barnardo

Tom Barnardo and his daughter Syrie, named after her mother.

Mossford Lodge c.1910. Mossford Lodge was originally gifted to Dr Barnardo upon his marriage. It became his first home for girls prior to the building of the Girls' Village Home at Barkingside.

Above: The original purpose-built houses which formed the Girls' Village Home at Barkingside. Among several uses, some of them now house administrative facilities for head office.

Inset: Fête at the Home, 1900s.

Facing page: Adoptive parent with Barnardo's worker and, *inset,* adopted son.

decided it would have to be closed. With its closure Syrie's official role in Barnardo's charity work ended – though she never failed to support her husband behind the scenes. Together they had seven children, three of whom died in early childhood and one of whom was mentally disabled. When Syrie co-edited her spouse's diaries after his death, she stressed what a wonderfully kind and tender husband he had been. But he can hardly have been an easy man to live with. He did not brook contradiction and never listened to argument. His word was law.

Though embarrassed by the closure of Mossford Lodge, Barnardo refused to admit defeat. Instead of a single large girls' home, he would build a girls' cottage village. He claimed the idea came to him – as many of his ideas did – in a dream. In fact the idea of running cottage homes for girls had originated on the Continent, and was already in operation elsewhere in England, but Barnardo may not have known that. He appealed for £13,500 to build a village of 30 cottages, each of which would house 20 girls – 600 in all. At first, fundraising for his new village was slow and desperately tough. But of course he persevered. Within two years he had enough confidence to ask Lord Aberdeen to lay the foundation stones, and in July 1876 Lord Cairns,

Top: Barnardo with two of his daughters, c.1895. The one on his back is Marjorie Elaine who had Down syndrome. It was through raising Marjorie that Dr Barnardo learnt a lot about children with special needs. His daughter Syrie stands behind.

Bottom: The Barnardo charter written on the side of the bridge that spans the Stepney Causeway, c.1910.

the Lord Chancellor, officiated at the opening of the first 14 cottages. It was yet another remarkable achievement. And Barnardo could now change his 'Ever Open Doors' slogan. Thenceforth it read: 'No Destitute Child Ever Refused Admission'.

Barnardo's lifestyle changed radically. He now had two homes, travelled by Hackney carriage, and employed servants. Rather than prowl the perilous East End streets at night himself, he employed beadles. His rise had been meteoric, and his success seemed unstoppable. But in the charity world, as everywhere else, success fuels envy and detractors. Tom Barnardo is not the only great charity worker whose achievements have been disparaged, even vilified. In recent times both Mother Theresa of Calcutta and Dr Albert Schweitzer in Africa have been attacked and defamed. Perhaps it goes with the territory. Maybe people who do so much good for others are bound to be mistrusted by the rest of us; perhaps their selflessness reminds us of our own selfishness more than is comfortable. In Tom Barnardo's case, his unshakeable conviction that his work was directly inspired by God, allied to his aggressive and often overbearing manner, gave him a self-confidence which frequently amounted to foolhardy arrogance. Though his charity's annual income was now around £25,000, he refused to work with either a committee or a treasurer. In consequence the publication of his Juvenile Mission's financial statements fell further and further behind. Though Barnardo was personally earning money writing for all he was worth, marriage had increased his personal financial difficulties, and Syrie was proving an extravagant money manager. Inevitably, people began to wonder about his lifestyle, and where the money he spent was coming from.

Two of those who most resented Barnardo's growing influence and affluence were Frederick Charrington and the Reverend George Reynolds. Charrington had been born into the wealthy brewing family, and had renounced his inheritance in order to become a charity worker himself, but he was far less successful than Barnardo; Reynolds was a Welsh Baptist Minister about whose background little is known. Charrington and Reynolds pooled their vindictive resources. Reynolds started the attack by circulating the scurrilous rumour that Barnardo, while a medical student, had had an improper relationship with his landlady, a Mrs Johnson. This story was rapidly shown to have no substance whatsoever. Barnardo demanded, and received, an apology from Reynolds. Charrington then joined the affray, and started to circulate the rumour again. Other stories hit the local press. Anonymous letters appeared in the *East London Observer*. The first, written by 'Diogenes', stressed Barnardo's lack of independent financial stewardship. The second, written by 'A Protestant Dissenter'

– actually George Reynolds – pulled no punches. It asked how Barnardo could afford his lifestyle: 'Dr Barnardo, instead of sacrificing all for the Lord's sake, has raised himself on the pedestal of his work.' Reynolds then suggested the Charity Organisation Society, which was well known to be hostile to Barnardo, should investigate his affairs.

The COS, as it was known, was a rather rudimentary predecessor of the Charity Commission. It had been launched in 1869 to bring some order and honesty to charity work in the East End. Like Andrew Carnegie, its members firmly believed in the historically accepted division between the 'deserving' and the 'undeserving' poor. The deserving were the lame, the halt, and the blind: those whose condition was beyond their own control. The undeserving were all the others, who were perceived to be the cause of their own misfortune. Barnardo could not have disagreed more. Most of his efforts, and his sympathies, were dedicated unswervingly to the children of the so-called undeserving poor.

DR. BARNARDO'S HOMES.

The nine "No's" which make the door of admission the Widest in the Wide World are:—

1. **No destitute Child refused.**
2. **No Race Barrier.**
3. **No Creed Clause.**
4. **No Physical Disability.**
5. **No Age limit.**
6. **No Money Promise.**
7. **No Voting.**
8. **No Waiting.**
9. **No Red Tape.**

The 'Nine No's' of Admission to Barnardo's, c.1880s

Dr Barnardo's had a strict appointments system controlled by his special clock shown here. At the start and finish of an appointment an ivory card would drop into view.

'Before and After'
photographs taken to
promote Barnardo's work,
and sold to raise money.
The fact that they were
carefully staged to
exaggerate the 'before and
after' effect aroused
controversy. But they were
fine examples of Barnardo's
innovative publicity, an
attribute of the charity
which continues today.

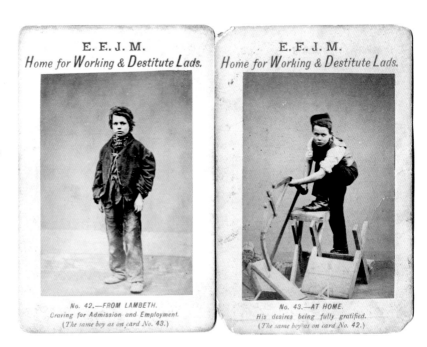

Barnardo responded to Reynolds' proposal by saying he would not be drawn into a public controversy. Reynolds stepped up his attack with more letters, one of which openly questioned Barnardo's right to the title of Doctor. Two extremely lengthy, discursive letters then appeared in the press supporting Barnardo, again published anonymously but widely thought to have been written by him in his own defence. Deciding that attack was the best means of defence, one of the letters even denied Charrington had ever really given up his inheritance. These letters caused a furore. Whoever wrote them – and

Barnardo always denied it was him – had stirred the pot too fiercely. After some further unpleasant exchanges between Barnardo and his antagonists, Reynolds brought matters to a head by publishing his charges against Barnardo under his own name, in a pamphlet with a title worthy of today's worst tabloid excesses: 'Dr Barnardo's Homes: Startling Revelations'. The pamphlet rehearsed all the old slurs, and added many more. There were specific charges of sexual abuse, of cruelty to children, of incompetent management, and of obtaining money under false pretences.

The last of these had some justification. One of Barnardo's most effective fundraising techniques was the publication of 'before' and 'after' photographs of the children he took into care. These photographs were simultaneously excellent propaganda for his cause, and were sold to raise money. The 'before' photographs naturally showed the poor children looking like unhappy pauper ragamuffins, the 'after' photographs showed them spruced up and cheerful. In his use of photography for publicity, as in so many other things, Barnardo was a pioneer. Many of these pairs of photographs survive, and are wonderful examples of early photographic art. Barnardo, however, was not always as scrupulous about them as he should have been. The pitiable appearances of the children in the 'before' pictures were exaggerated, as were their neat and tidy appearances afterwards. Not many years later movie stars and others (including charities) would be using such techniques routinely, but their use in Victorian philanthropic advertising was unwise. Tom Barnardo would certainly have believed the end justified the means: a little exaggeration was insignificant compared with the need to raise funds for destitute children. But his opponents were able to turn this practice against him.

During 1875 the public controversy, and the ceaseless attacks upon him, began to bite. Barnardo's health suffered badly, but even more importantly – from his point of view – donations began to plummet. By then he had six hundred children in his care. The following year was the most troubled and traumatic of Thomas John Barnardo's life.

Responding to the pressure, Barnardo at last appointed a committee of trustees. He intensely disliked giving up total personal control of his operation, but in the event it was the trustees – all friends and supporters – who extradited him from the parlous situation in which he found himself. They interviewed him at length, to assure themselves of his innocence on all charges. Then they managed his defence, with considerable skill and wisdom. They appointed auditors. They got the COS – despite its hostility to Barnardo – to

Barnardo's children made shoes – like this original shoe.

agree to the setting up of an arbitration inquiry to resolve matters. They raised much of the money (though not quite enough) to pay for his defence. At the end of the arbitration Barnardo was left with a personal debt of £2,400, and for many years thereafter was in serious financial straits.

After a long and painful investigation, in October 1877 the arbitrators published their report. From all of the most serious charges Barnardo was completely exonerated. As far as the rumours circulated by Reynolds and Charrington were concerned the arbitrators wrote: 'these statements, with few exceptions . . . were not justifiable, having at the first been made without due enquiry, and having been subsequently unsupported by evidence.' With regard to Barnardo's use of the title 'Doctor' the COS took a fairly relaxed view, as he had by then obtained his licentiate from the Royal College of Surgeons in Edinburgh, though they added that it was 'strictly true he had no legal or real right to the title and style of Doctor'. They were extremely critical of his use of misleading photographs, and he never used such photographs again. Finally, and crucially, the arbitrators stated unequivocally that defamatory articles and publications, produced by either side, must cease. Despite the arbitrators' report, however, some of the mud inevitably stuck. Even Lord Shaftesbury wrote: 'Is it a just acquittal? If so I rejoice. But if he was guilty I lament that iniquity has triumphed.'

The arbitration marks another watershed in Barnardo's life. Beforehand, he had been relatively unknown outside the East End, and been wholly independent. Now he was a public figure, answering to trustees and auditors, and above all saddled with debt. Ever since joining the Plymouth Brethren in his teens he had accepted their tenet 'owe no man anything'. Now he could no longer live by that tenet. He felt he had to withdraw from the Brethren. He joined the Church of England. But the loss of his Brethren friends added to his personal anguish. Fortunately for him, he was helped and supported throughout this period by Lord Cairns, the Lord Chancellor, who made it known that Barnardo's Homes was very much his favourite charity. And Cairns was Disraeli's favourite minister: a powerful ally.

The trauma of the arbitration case and its attendant anxieties slowly receded. Barnardo learned to work with his trustees, who set up a rota to visit the homes. Barnardo was required to supply information about all the children in care every month in great detail, including full medical reports. From having been amateurishly well-meaning, Barnardo's homes were now being run more professionally than others. Expansion continued apace. The number of Village Homes for girls increased; Lady Cairns' niece gave Barnardo a property in Jersey,

A tinted postcard of Babies'
Castle at Hawkhurst, Kent.

which he turned into a convalescent home for sick boys; another
supporter made over a building in Hawkhurst, which Barnardo chris-
tened 'Babies Castle' because he cared for tiny abandoned infants
there. And in the 1880s he began his child emigration policy. Soon
parties of toddlers and children were leaving from Liverpool each
spring, to the accompaniment of bands playing, hymn singing,
banner waving and tumultuous cheers: Barnardo always put on a
tremendous show. Though he was certainly aware of the risks,
Barnardo felt the squalid conditions in which many children were
living in London to be so appalling that almost nothing could be
worse. Nonetheless he was far from negligent about the emigrant

The Teighmore home, Jersey,
with two members of staff
standing outside, 1900s.

children's care. His first investigative visit to Canada in 1884 lasted more than three months. He returned to a boisterous welcome from a congregation of over 4,000 at the Edinburgh Castle. And in 1886 he introduced his system of boarding out: fostering.

Children of both sexes were boarded out, but fostering with suitably respectable families was especially appropriate for destitute girls. In return for their care they provided domestic help. Barnardo also saw, far-sightedly, that for illegitimate children foster homes were better than orphanages. The care of illegitimate children had long been an intractable problem, for both state and charitable institutions. It was feared that taking illegitimate children into care condoned licentious sexual behaviour – indeed encouraged it. (What woman would not behave wickedly, the righteous asked, if she were free to dump her illegitimate offspring on others?) Moreover, illegitimate children in institutional homes were likely to be bullied and treated especially badly by other children. As long as the foster parents were willing and understanding, Barnardo saw that boarding out would be an ideal solution to this long-running dilemma. The children, often no more than babies, were taken into a foster family, and the mothers went into service nearby. It must be added, however, that even Dr Barnardo allowed an unmarried mother only one mistake. If she became pregnant a second time the first child was instantly yanked out of its foster home: obviously taking care of the infant had, indeed, encouraged the girl to keep behaving wantonly.

Though Barnardo never completed his medical studies, he never sloughed off his medical heritage. To mark Queen Victoria's Golden Jubilee, he built Her Majesty's Hospital for Sick Children as part of the Stepney development, at a cost of £7,800. It was three-and-a-half storeys high and contained six general wards, plus isolation and convalescent wards, with seventy cots. It also contained an operating theatre, and was one of the first hospitals to focus exclusively on children's diseases. By the standards of the time hygiene was excellent and the mortality rate was exceptionally low. It was another triumph of Barnardo's vision: by the beginning of the twentieth century it was the largest children's hospital in London.

His charitable work expanded and deepened. Emigration and boarding out enabled him to triple the number of children in his care during the next five years. By the end of the 1880s the annual income from donations was in excess of £100,000. But despite these successes, Barnardo was never long out of trouble. He attracted good and bad publicity in about equal measure. When the National Society for the Prevention of Cruelty to Children was formed in 1884, he was a founding member. A few years later he publicly broke with the NSPCC, because he believed it had been infiltrated by Roman

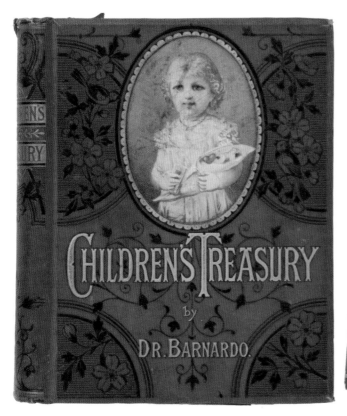

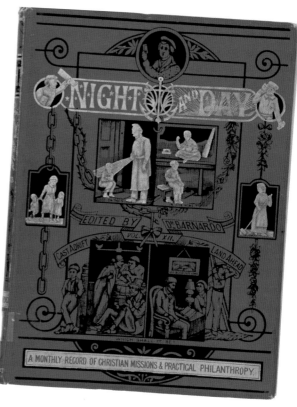

Catholics, of whom – being an Irish Protestant – he had a deep and abiding mistrust. In 1889 another long and exhausting battle broke out when the Catholic parents of three children in Barnardo's care demanded their offspring be returned to them. (One of the three children had earlier been sold by his mother to a couple of organ grinders she met in a pub, who treated the boy as their 'monkey'.) Barnardo promptly bundled two of the children out of the country in such a way that they could not be traced, and applied to the courts to retain custody of the third. As a consequence, for the next three years Barnardo was mired in litigation with the parents, as they attempted to regain their children. He fought all three cases in the High Court, and two went to the House of Lords. He righteously believed he was protecting the children from dreadful parents – but he was also keen to stop them being brought up as Roman Catholics. Predictably, public opinion turned against him. He was accused of 'kidnapping' the children and sustained more widespread abuse and criticism than at any other time in his career.

It can hardly be surprising that all this litigation, in tandem with Barnardo's indomitable expansionist drive – fuelled by his 'Ever Open Doors' policy – put the charity under substantial fiscal strain. The cracks had already begun to show in the annual report for 1889, shortly before the cases of the three Catholic children began. In that year Barnardo persuaded the trustees

Barnardo founded two successful magazines, *The Children's Treasury* and *Night and Day*, principally to publicise his charitable work.

that the homes in Stepney, Jersey and Hawkhurst needed to be rebuilt. He was always determined that the children's buildings should be as pleasant as they possibly could be – a great tradition that continues in Barnardo's to this day. But the rebuilding meant new mortgages had to be created and new overdrafts arranged. At the same time, Barnardo decided provincial centres had to be opened, in Bath, Cardiff, Edinburgh, Leeds, Liverpool, Newcastle and Plymouth, to cope with the growing problem of child destitution outside London. Again his trustees agreed. By 1892 the number of children in care had risen to over 4,000 – and Barnardo's debts multiplied. The South Western Bank wrote to say they were owed £18,000, and a further overdraft of £22,000 was arranged against the deeds of Barnardo properties. £10,000 was borrowed from the UK Temperance Provident Society. And so the debts mounted.

Barnardo's finances were weakened still further by his insistence on caring for sick and disabled children. Not surprisingly, the children of the poor suffered from a plethora of terrible illnesses: rickets, inherited syphilis, polio, tuberculosis and other respiratory diseases, curved spines and other deformities. Barnardo had announced plans to establish a special home for disabled children in 1875, but he did not manage to open the home until 1887. He vacillated and wavered about the desirability, or otherwise, of segregating disabled children from others, but always veered towards integration. Unquestionably, he found the care of disabled children the most rewarding work he undertook, and he worked at it passionately, his medical knowledge making him especially effective. Equally, this work was especially costly, and ran him further into debt. As always, Barnardo refused to allow money difficulties to deter him.

Desperate for funds, in 1893 Barnardo wrote in his magazine *Night and Day*:

> *A great crisis has arisen in the history of our work – a crisis the gravity of which cannot easily be exaggerated . . . I stand face to face with the most serious problem which has ever met me in my twenty-seven years of labour among destitute children . . .*

Although the initial response was encouraging, it soon petered out, well short of the £10,000 the trustees felt was needed. At last his trustees put their foot down. Less relief work was to be undertaken. Barnardo's publications were slimmed down; the number of new children admitted was reduced, as was the number boarded out. Only the number of children sent abroad continued to grow. But the total number of children helped in 1892 was not reached again until 1899, when the charity was legally incorporated, and the trustees were protected from its debts by limited liability. Thereafter, the trustees saw no reason to restrain Barnardo's work. When Dr Barnardo died in 1905 the charity's liabilities totalled £249,000.

Though he never lost faith that God would provide him with the means to carry on his work, Barnardo understandably began to find the need to beg for money increasingly wearisome. However none of this detracted from his love of grand showmanship. In 1890 he hired the Royal Albert Hall for the charity's annual meeting, which was attended by nearly 7,000 people. The event proved so successful that he began to put on regular shows there – from 1894 onwards he was mounting two a year, another immense workload. And in 1896 he chose the Royal Albert Hall for the charity's thirtieth anniversary celebration.

No effort was spared to make this celebration an awesomely spectacular event. The Prince and Princess of Wales, later to become King Edward VII and Queen Alexandra, agreed to preside. Over 3,000 Barnardo's children took part. Every aspect of the charity's work was represented on stage: at one moment the centre of the hall was filled with working lads in their industrial rig out, minutes later babies in

A rehearsal for the Annual Display at the Albert Hall, 1900, demonstrating trades by boys from the Stepney home. Dr Barnardo is on the rostrum, directing the rehearsal; girls from the Girls' Village Home are in the choir seats; Stepney boys are in the band in the centre.

cots filled the space, followed by a party of boys and girls en route for Canada and dressed for the journey, then there was a display of life and work at the Ilford Girls' Village Home, and a disabled children's cricket match. (To have kept the disabled children away would have been to admit they were inferior, Barnardo said, anticipating criticism.) Finally the stage was filled with 400 grateful old boys and girls. The Prince of Wales spoke, and Barnardo rounded things off with an appeal for funds. Yet despite the brilliance of the event, and despite the Hall being full to capacity, the response to the appeal was disappointing.

Nonetheless, Dr Barnardo continued to drive himself still harder. In 1904 he opened a sanatorium for young consumptives close by the Girls' Village Home. He now often worked at home, but employed relays of support staff, and rarely finished before midnight. He dictated documents endlessly, and kept a small corps of typewriters busy. To keep himself going he drank strong black tea. Though he had always been a hearty eater he often had no time for meals, and would put himself to bed after midnight with a beef sandwich which had been held in a book press so that the juices seeped into the bread – one of his own inventions – and in his twilight days he would pour himself a quick drink. Not a lot of people knew that. Nor was it as hypocritical as it may sound: Barnardo preached against the evils of alcohol in excess, not against the occasional bedtime snifter.

He was now suffering from deafness, repeated attacks of angina and a weakening constitution. To recuperate from the angina attacks he made several trips to the spa at Bad Neuheim near Frankfurt. These provided transient relief, but it was clear his heath was failing, and his condition was not improved when he was involved in a railway accident in 1904, even though he was not himself physically injured.

His trustee committee was by now making determined efforts to gain public recognition for his work. A letter signed by 48 eminent personalities was published in *The Times* under the heading 'A Claim Upon The Nation', in which they asked for £120,000 to pay off what was believed to be the charity's debt. (The true extent of the debt was not discovered until after Dr Barnardo's death.)

In August 1905 Barnardo again set out for Bad Neuheim, but on the way he was taken ill in Cologne. His wife Syrie, together with one of his brothers and one of his sons, went out to bring him home. He returned on 14 September, suffered further intensely painful attacks and died, still working, the next week. He was 60.

The following morning the nation's newspapers carried long obituaries, praising him for his philanthropy and his care of homeless children, and marvelling at the extent of his achievements. *The Times* wrote: 'It is impossible not to be astonished by the magnitude of his

The Barnardos with their daughter Marjorie c.1895.

work . . . he raised up a noble monument of philanthropy and usefulness.' *The Manchester Evening Chronicle* said: 'He has left behind him such an enduring monument to noble self sacrificing effort, such a legacy of good deeds well done, such a claim upon the reverence of the nation as few men among us will leave'. His friends mourned both for him and for the fact that so few similar words of praise had been published during his lifetime – during which he had been forced constantly to fight for recognition and appreciation.

The King and Queen sent their condolences to Syrie. The funeral cortège travelled from the East End of London to the Girls' Village Home accompanied everywhere by grieving crowds. At the Girls' Village a colossal marquee had to be erected to accommodate the vast number of mourners. The coffin lay in state first in the Edinburgh Castle and then near the Girls' Village to enable the public to pay its respects. And a cinefilm was made of the funeral procession – one of the first news movies ever made.

During his lifetime Thomas John Barnardo cared for 59,384 children. (The precision of the figure reflects the care he devoted to keeping accurate records.) Of these over 23,000 had been boarded out. At the time of his death more than half of some 8,000 children in his care were being boarded out; the rest lived in 43 homes around the country. And of the 8,000 over 1,300 were disabled. In the Girls' Village, which had become his most beloved Home, there were now 65 cottages housing 1,250 girls. His personal influence on the upbringing of destitute children had spread as far as Japan, China, India, Australia, Argentina and North America. In the first year of his work the charity's income had been £214.15s.0d. in 1905 the charity's income was £196,286.11s.0d. – and over those years more than £3,000,000 had been collected and spent. Despite the contradictions

in his life, the two great principles upon which his charity work was built never wavered: no destitute child should ever be refused admission, and children of whatever ethnicity or nationality, irrespective of any physical infirmity, should be eligible. In adhering to those two principles Tom Barnardo's foresight, and his humanity, were unrivalled.

After his death many serious commentators remarked that, noble and impressive though his life's work had been, it should never have been necessary. The state, through its various agencies, should have looked after the tens of thousands of poor, orphaned and infirm children who – without Dr Barnardo – would have been left to roam the streets, by day and by night. Today, a century after his death, it is estimated that there are still 33,000 homeless youngsters aged 16-21 in Britain. So much for progress.

Today Barnardo's directly helps over 100,000 children each year – more than ten times as many as Tom Barnardo helped at his peak. The philanthropic work he began continues unabated.

The funeral procession passing through Liverpool Street, London, 1905.

The 20th Century: Winds of Change

4

Dr Thomas Barnardo was so powerful a figure, and had run his charity so autocratically, that it is perhaps not surprising that for many years after his death little changed. Despite, or maybe because of, the demands he put upon them, most of Dr Barnardo's staff were steadfastly loyal to him, and their loyalty endured. Those who had known him personally – and even those who had not – constantly looked over their shoulders, worrying about what he would or would not have done, what he would or would not have wanted. Some of those who had known him were still working for Barnardo's when the Second World War broke out in 1939. For them, to alter any of 'The Doctor's Schemes' was tantamount to sacrilege. For these reasons, and for organisational reasons to which we will return, throughout the first half of the twentieth century the charity was slow to adjust to new circumstances. Far from welcoming progress and change, the organisation tried determinedly to resist them.

Adoption, for example, was legalised in 1926, but for over 20 years Barnardo's would have none of it. Why? Partly because the trustees were suspicious of its long-term effects, but mostly because the founder had always insisted Barnardo's was itself the children's – even the boarded out children's – surrogate 'family'. Adoption would give them a different family. This was unacceptable. Over the years, some Barnardo's foster parents had adopted their foster-children privately, almost surreptitiously, but it was not until after the Curtis Report strongly advocated the benefits of adoption in 1946 that Barnardo's bowed to public pressure, becoming a registered adoption society the following year. As so often in the history of Barnardo's, in the long run the founder's instincts have not proved altogether wrong. The Curtis Report was followed during the 1950s and 1960s by a helter-skelter rush into adoption. Throughout the country some 500,000 children were adopted, and many of them were badly misplaced. Barnardo's was more cautious. And the charity tried to keep in touch with all the children whose adoption it had organised, just as it has always tried to keep in touch with every member of its

Vocational training has always been an important function, although careers and methods have changed radically during the century.

Main picture: An instructor at the Russell-Cotes Naval School describing rigging details on a model boat to a group of Barnardo's boys.

Above: Food technology is one of today's popular subjects.

hugely extended 'family'. Modern knowledge of post-adoption stress has shown that this kind of long-term relationship can be highly beneficial for adopted children.

After Dr Barnardo's death the children's lives in the residential homes became, if anything, even more austere. Tom Barnardo, stern disciplinarian though he was, tempered his discipline with kindness. Once he was gone, many of those who ran the homes applied his strictures by rote. Their regimens were severe, and sometimes cruel. Here, for example, are the words of ex-Barnardo girl Janet Hitchman who, as we saw earlier, wrote so enthusiastically about her preference for residential homes over fostering. Nonetheless, looking back she said:

> *There have been some remarkable personalities among the thousands who have worked in the Homes. Not all of them unfortunately reached the high ideals of the founder. It is difficult to understand why some of them stayed so long in work to which they were not suited, among children they obviously disliked . . . probably their harshness was in part due to their inability to keep order in any other way.*

All the same, Barnardo's continued to do an immense amount of good for children after the founder's death. More and more children were taken into care, and new homes were continually being opened to house them. Reflecting this expansion, the charity officially changed its name to Dr Barnardo's Homes – somewhat misleadingly, and more than somewhat regrettably, in view of the many other services Barnardo's provided. Residential care reached its peak in the 1930s: in 1933 Barnardo's had over 8000 children living in 188 homes – both figures more than double the levels of 1905. In part this growth reflected a dwindling number of children being boarded out. It was as though the charity's Council and managers, like everyone else, had bought into the misconception that Dr Barnardo himself had just run homes – though this, as we have seen, was far from the truth. Towards the end of his life Barnardo had become utterly convinced well-organised fostering was, for most children, superior to living in a residential home. For many decades his successors did not seem to see things that way.

Throughout his life Dr Barnardo had dreamed, like Lord Shaftesbury, of running residential training ships for boys. It was one of the few dreams he never quite realised. Although he drew up the detailed plans, he did not live to see the official opening of his Watts Naval Training School in April 1906, which accommodated 320 boys. During the First World War many Watts boys served in the Royal Navy with great distinction, winning praise for the school from the

Admiralty itself. Building on this success, in 1919 Barnardo's opened the Russell-Cotes School for Nautical Seamen, in Dorset, which was about half the size of Watts. From 1903 to 1946 the cover of all but four of Barnardo's Annual Reports showed a wistful sailor boy bearing a Union Jack on which was emblazoned the inscription 'For God and Country'. Barnardo's continued to train young seamen until 1964, by which time naval careers had long ceased to have much appeal for most boys – and anyway fewer boys were needed by the navy.

Meanwhile Barnardo's had tried to replicate the success of the Girls' Village Home at Ilford by acquiring a 39-acre estate in Woodford Bridge, Essex. The aim was to accommodate 900 boys in 30 smallish cottages, though this number was never achieved. The Boys' Garden City, as it was named, was officially opened by Her Royal Highness the Duchess of Albany. As well as opening its doors to new needy children, the Garden City welcomed many from Barnardo's old homes in the East End, which were well past their best. Then in 1922 the trustees bought Goldings, a pseudo-Elizabethan pile standing in 50 acres near Hertford, to accommodate yet a further 300 boys. Goldings was opened by the Prince of Wales, and a year later Queen Mary visited the Girls' Village Home in Ilford.

A group of boys practising their knot tying, 1934.

Two boys sitting on top of the newly erected sign board at the entrance to the gate of The William Baker Technical School, Goldings, 1922.

Bootmaking shop at Goldings, 1920s.

Boys watering the gardens at the Boys' Village Home.

Barnardo's Windermere Construction Skills service provides training for young people with special education needs.

Below: Actor Andy Serkis, 'Gollum' of *Lord of the Rings* fame, and his wife, actress Lorraine Ashbourne, at Barnardo's Spark Centre in Bethnal Green, London, to mark the opening of a new IT suite.

Her Majesty The Queen waves goodbye as she leaves her children's tea party at Buckingham Palace. Royalty have made a massive contribution to the charity's funds.

Above right: Princess Margaret attended the centenary birthday party at the Royal Albert Hall in 1966 where she received posies from Barnardo's Young Helpers and watched performances by the children.

It is a mark of Barnardo's high standing that since the end of the nineteenth century many senior members of royalty and the nobility have willingly associated themselves with its work. Four Kings, four Queens and one Princess have been Patrons of Barnardo's. HM Queen Elizabeth the Queen Mother was Patron for over 60 years. Both HRH Princess Margaret and Diana Princess of Wales were Presidents of Barnardo's. This is a tradition which continues. HM The Queen is Patron today. Its royal supporters have helped raise a small fortune for the charity.

Goldings' formal name was the William Baker Technical School, named after the director of the charity who took over after Dr Barnardo's death in 1905. The 'technical school' in the name emphasised another Barnardo's tradition. It reflected a growing belief within Barnardo's that one of the founder's most important contributions to childcare was his commitment to vocational training. By 1939 the boys at Goldings, instead of learning the trades of the founder's time, were being trained as motor mechanics and electricians. This too is a tradition which continues. At High Close School in Wokingham, for example, children with behavioural difficulties are nowadays taught culinary skills – and they love it. Several High Close leavers have already become successful chefs.

While accommodation in homes was growing apace, emigration to Canada also continued, though its wisdom was increasingly being questioned, both within Barnardo's and without. In 1913 the Barnardo's Council had serious misgivings about emigration, sparked off by the behaviour of one of its managers in Canada, who was later found to be co-habiting with a girl in his care. Many important developments in childcare have been prompted by such scandals and tragedies. It is as though governments and the public are happy to forget about children in care until something forces them to pay attention – while ordinary children should be seen and not heard, vulnerable children should best be forgotten about.

Barnardo's miscreant manager in Canada was ousted and things were put right, but the case spotlit the inescapable perils of long-distance childcare. In 1924 Ramsay MacDonald's Government sent over a delegation, which reported very unfavourably on the emigration of children under 14 – though quite favourably on the emigration of older ones. The Canadian government promptly banned the immigration of under-14s, and in 1939 stopped taking lone children at all. By that time 20,699 destitute boys and 8,377 girls had been shipped across the Atlantic by Barnardo's alone.

From the 1920s onwards Barnardo's also sent children to Australia, though the depression of the 1930s dampened the Australians' enthusiasm for poor immigrant children, and the numbers that went to the Antipodes never came anywhere near equalling those that crossed the Atlantic. By 1965 just 2,784 boys and girls had been sent to Australia, where Barnardo's had built ten small homes and a training farm in New South Wales.

In 1967 all child emigration ceased for good.

Meanwhile, in the UK, the medical treatment that Barnardo's provided to the children in its care was constantly improving, and indeed was one of the charity's finest services: yet another Barnardo's

The Princess of Wales was a President of Barnardo's.

Nowadays High Close School in Wokingham provides for children with special educational needs.

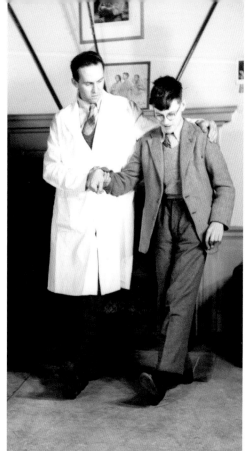

Above: Physiotherapy at Warlies, 1957.

Above right: Warlies building in Waltham Abbey, Essex, 1941/42. Warlies was opened in 1927 as a girls' training home. In 1940 it was converted into a vocational girls' domestic training school. In 1954 it became a mixed school for children with physical disabilities.

tradition stemming from Dr Barnardo himself, though with the advent of the National Health Service it is not one that functions in the same way today. But in 1908 an advanced X-ray unit was installed in Her Majesty's Hospital in Stepney, and in the same year the first dentist joined the medical staff. In 1923 Barnardo's Stepney infirmary was replaced by a spanking new hospital at Woodford Bridge, which again was in the van when it launched a children's physiotherapy unit shortly after opening. By 1937 Barnardo's was running two 100-bed hospitals for children, with outpatients and massage departments, plus four convalescent homes. During the 1930s, despite the economic recession, Barnardo's made a further outstanding contribution to poor children's health by sponsoring a great deal of original research into children's illnesses. Youngsters in Barnardo's care generally received far better medical treatment than other poor children – treatment that was often better than wealthy children received, for that matter.

Dr Barnardo's successors' handling of physically and mentally handicapped children was perhaps less satisfactory. Though he had at first been in two minds about the issue, Tom Barnardo had come to believe that the integration and acceptance of handicapped children must be vigorously encouraged. In this he had, once again, been quite remarkably progressive. But the cost of looking after such children had always been steep, particularly for a charity chronically short of funds. Nonetheless, Barnardo himself had been characteristically resolute. At the time of his death 13% of the children in his care were disabled. By 1925 the figure had fallen to only 5%. In 1928 Warlies, a stately home near Waltham Abbey, was acquired. It was to accommodate 53 mentally disabled girls who had been living in the Girls' Village Home – a segregation the founder would have deplored. This was one of the few areas in which his successors defied the founder's principles. They were unwise. Warlies was not a success. In 1940 it was converted into a vocational girls' domestic training school. Barnardo's did not attempt to care for children with learning difficulties again for another 20 years.

All these developments, and many more, to a greater or lesser extent sustained – and mostly built upon – Tom Barnardo's foundations. But the 1930s brought the first inklings of fundamental change. As a result of the great depression many previously affluent families, perhaps for the first time in history in such numbers, found themselves in penury. And for the first time Barnardo's found itself looking after children who had, until the crash, been living reasonably affluent lives. These children were not accustomed to the restrictions and harsh disciplines of Barnardo's life. Frank Norman, author of *Fings Ain't Wot They Used T' Be*, and who was an illegitimate and far from affluent child, was sent to a Barnardo's home in 1937, aged seven. He stayed with Barnardo's for nine years, and he did not enjoy it much. In his autobiography 'Banana Boy' he describes the daily schedule:

> *Month followed month and year followed year uneventfully, just the same old institutional routine, day in day out. Get up, wash, make your bed, sweep the floor, breakfast, PT, morning prayers, classes, lunch, play, tea, mow the lawn, play, evening prayers (God bless all except the wall), bed, sleep. Except for Sundays the only way to tell which day of the week it was was by what we were having for lunch. The menu never changed from one year's end to the next, but we seemed to thrive on it, though perhaps it would be better to say we survived on it.*

It is hardly surprising that this regime appealed even less to children coming from previously well-off families than it did to Frank Norman. In Dr Barnardo's time the boys' day had started at 5.30am and ended with lights out at 10.00pm. By the 1930s this schedule had been relaxed a little – the day usually started at 6.30am. In the Stepney Causeway home, boys were still summoned for 'tooth inspection' by a bugle call every day.

The new intake had little in common with the homes' more traditional residents. They were as immiscible as posh prisoners in a rough jail. Each group of children was foreign to the other. The middle-class children were less tough, and less good at fisticuffs and fighting. But they were also more articulate, and had been accustomed to much

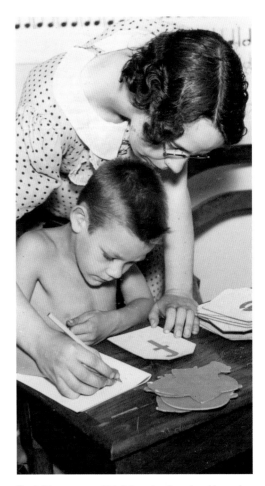

Frank Norman as a child doing school work at Howard House, Bedford, 1937.

Warlies girls domestic training school, laundry, 1945.

73

freer ways of living. As well as being ill equipped to cope with the rigours of impoverished, regimented life, they were personally conscious of the need to find appropriate careers. Traditionally Barnardo's children were relatively grateful to be trained for any job at all. The new boys did not wish to learn to be skilled manual workers, nor did the girls aspire to a life in domestic service. The new intake exerted pressure for things to change. As the perceptive Janet Hitchman wrote of that period: 'The homes were changed much more from within than through any government report.'

The depressed 1930s slid inexorably into the Second World War. Barnardo's had emerged from the First World War relatively unscathed and unchanged. Many ex-Barnardo's boys served in the armed forces with valour, and many were decorated. In 1916 a Zeppelin shell had fallen on the Girls' Village lawn in Ilford, but no great harm was done. During the 1914-18 War funds were especially short, income down, and salaries were kept so low that even the most loyal staff considered leaving. But a constant flow of generous food parcels arrived for the

Warlies girls domestic training school cookery class, 1945.

Dr B's Kitchen, Belfast, trains young people with learning disabilities. Its restaurant is open to the public.

Evacuees from Barnardo's Girls
Village Home in 1940.

children from the Empire, and the old Barnardo's order somehow overcame the difficulties.

In contrast the Second World War, and its immediate aftermath, accelerated the changes the 1930s had begun. Taken as a whole, the 1940s were a watershed both for Barnardo's and for the progress of childcare in Britain. Wartime evacuation intensified the process of amalgamating children from different social classes. Boys and girls from Barnardo's homes were sent off to live with families from other social strata, in safer parts of the country, while the government requisitioned the evacuated Barnardo's buildings for war purposes. This in turn forced the charity to work more closely than had previously been its wont with outside bodies – government agencies, local authorities and other voluntary organisations. It forced Barnardo's out of its protective shell.

It wasn't only the War that enforced changes. In 1940 and 1941 two Ministry of Health reports severely criticised one of Barnardo's long-established homes, and threatened to close it down. It was a mixed-sex home in County Durham, where an 18-year-old girl had become pregnant by a Barnardo's boy. The ensuing scandal stung the Barnardo's Council into action: another example of outrage catalysing change. The Durham home was promptly converted into a single-sex institution, for boys only. Then in October 1941 the first Barnardo's staff training school was opened, at Woodford Bridge.

From its inception the new staff-training school ran courses in childcare and welfare, child psychology, hygiene, first aid and nursing, children's hobbies, games, and Bible storytelling. Barnardo's was becoming committed to a new professionalism. For the first time a professional social worker, who had worked with London County Council, was put in charge of boarding out – an area of activity which had run into particular difficulty during the evacuation chaos at the start of the War. Then in 1944 the first *Barnardo's Book* was published. Nothing like it had been seen in Barnardo's before. It was a detailed manual which gave the staff specific instructions on how to behave in every conceivable circumstance, and simultaneously sought to curb the rigid routines in the homes. It encouraged an altogether more relaxed attitude among the children ('Complete silence is not desirable, and savours of Institution rather than home . . . The ideal home is a place where each member feels secure in the kindliness and affection of the others . . .'). *The Barnardo's Book* introduced precise rules concerning, and restricting, the use of punishment. By inference at least, the book strongly implied that life in the homes had previously been harsh and repressive. From the time of its publication until the last Barnardo's long-term residential home was finally closed some four decades later, life for the decreasing

Adoption shop in Colchester. Pictures of the children needing adoption were displayed in the windows.

skilled but willing volunteers to look after toddlers, highly trained and qualified professionals to look after the children with learning difficulties and mental health problems. Children and families of all races and creeds were equally welcome, and they worked and played together in the same units. In Barnardo's printed literature, where not so long before there had been no coverage whatsoever of black and Asian children, photographs of multiracial groups of kids were now to be seen in abundance. Some of Barnardo's new work was carried out directly in partnership with government agencies, some was carried out under contract from government agencies, and all of it was carried out with the approval of the relevant government agencies.

In 1983 the Annual Report was able finally to state: 'This year has seen the closure of the last of our old-style Barnardo's children's homes.' During the previous century Barnardo's had housed no fewer than 350,000 children, many of whom looked back on their years in Barnardo's homes with great affection. But those days had passed, and were gone forever. In the 1960s and 1970s more than 90 homes had been closed. The children in them had to be found new places to live; the staff could often not be found new jobs and so were made redundant. Barnardo's was now committed only to short-term and highly specialised residential work, helping severely disabled children, or children with extreme behavioural or learning difficulties, or children living in residences with their families.

In the 1990s the Barnardo's net spread still wider. New projects were initiated to handle the growing challenge of sexual abuse, especially to help young girls and boys abused through prostitution, and to help children affected by HIV/AIDS. More projects were spread around the country. Child homelessness resurfaced, and Barnardo's

This and facing page:
Playscheme for children
with learning disabilities,
Harrogate, 1980.

helped vagrant children cope with their psychological and emotional problems. There was an increasing need to find adoptive and foster homes for children of non-UK origin – some of Afro-Caribbean or Asian origin, others fleeing from war-torn, ravaged areas of Europe. And Barnardo's started work on the complex task of evaluating the success and long-term effectiveness of its own activities. With so much public money involved, whether coming from donors or from taxation, Barnardo's began to make strenuous efforts to be sure that every penny was being spent to good effect.

Barnardo's also increased its commitment to social and political campaigning, recognising that more can and should be done by government, and by society as a whole, to alleviate the appalling disadvantages under which so many children still live. There is a limit to the amount any charity, no matter how large, can do on its own. The 1948 Children Act placed the responsibility for looking after the UK's children squarely on the nation's shoulders, but the nation has not yet fully woken up to this responsibility. The election of the Labour government in 1997 marked the start of a remarkable growth in government expenditure on the social services – and with it a rapid growth in Barnardo's work. The number of children Barnardo's helped climbed from 30,000 in 1997 to more than 50,000 in 1999 – an increase of well over 60% in little more than two years. The figure has since more than doubled again.

The end of the twentieth century also saw the launch of a new long-term advertising drive, designed to reposition Barnardo's in the public mind. The public had resolutely hung on to its old-fashioned image of Barnardo's as a charity that runs orphanages. To put across the truth, Barnardo's started a provocative and impactful advertising campaign, which has engendered a great deal of public comment – as was intended.

But does it really matter if the public has misconceptions about what Barnardo's does?

For several reasons, it matters a lot. Fairly or unfairly, today many people have a negative view of the old 'orphanages', so they are unlikely to give money to a charity which runs them; equally, the image of running orphanages clouds – indeed sometimes obliterates completely – the vast quantity of modern and important work Barnardo's currently undertakes, which undoubtedly deserves wide public support; moreover it is unhelpful to the staff, the authorities and the children themselves for the charity's work to be so wrongly perceived. In the long run a charity cannot survive without public support. Barnardo's allowed the misunderstandings about its work to continue unchecked for many decades. It became clear that these misconceptions were never going to right themselves of their own accord. That is why Barnardo's started, and still continues, its often contentious advertising. Market research shows that, slowly, the public is getting the right message.

At the end of the twentieth century Barnardo's defined six clear building blocks upon which all future work would be built. Barnardo's stated that every child deserves, and needs:

- a family that can cope
- protection from harm
- emotional, physical and mental health
- a sense of belonging in the community
- opportunities to learn
- a stake in society.

The charity also adopted new vision and purpose statements: Barnardo's vision is that all children and young people should be free from poverty, abuse and discrimination. Barnardo's purpose is to help the most vulnerable children and young people transform their lives and fulfil their potential.

All of this was a million miles in practice, but only a few millimetres in intention, from the great philanthropic work Tom Barnardo started in Stepney well over 100 years ago. During the twentieth century, everything had changed – and nothing had changed.

The 21st Century:
A Kaleidoscopic Quilt

5

It is perhaps unwise to describe a charity as 'thriving'. It might suggest the charity has lots of money, maybe too much, and finds its work altogether too agreeable, perhaps even fun. Barnardo's is thriving, but certainly does not have too much money, and nobody who visits a Barnardo's project could possibly come away thinking that working with vulnerable children is exactly fun. Tremendously satisfying, without a doubt – as it was for Dr Barnardo himself. Wonderfully rewarding – few things can be more rewarding than having a small child grin happily in response to your help and loving care. And though playing with Barnardo's kids can be hugely entertaining, forever lurking in the back of the mind of every Barnardo's worker is the nagging knowledge that something about the life of each child in their care is horribly wrong – otherwise the child would not be there.

Barnardo's today is thriving in the sense that it has been growing, which means it has been able to help more and more children each year; it is trusted by government agencies to do excellent work; it is highly respected, even if still misunderstood; it has a wonderful team of dedicated and immeasurably hardworking staff and volunteers; it manages to combine tradition with innovation, constantly striving to find new ways to help children more effectively; and it receives countless significant and generous donations from the public – even if those donations are never quite sufficient to do all the work Barnardo's knows needs to be done.

In the first few years of the twenty-first century, the number of children directly helped by Barnardo's has grown spectacularly, from 50,000 to over 100,000 annually. The number of caring projects run by the charity nationwide has increased from around 300 to over 360. Its total charitable expenditure has increased from £119 million to a current almost £200 million. Inevitably, the number of staff employed to do this huge volume of work has grown too, from nearly 5,000 to well over 6,000 – not to mention the army of volunteers.

Today Barnardo's operations are like a vast, kaleidoscopic quilt which covers nooks and crannies all over Britain where vulnerable and disadvantaged children need help. As will become apparent,

Above: Volunteers have raised funds by running for Barnardo's, both in the UK and overseas.

Main picture: Toddlers party, Barnardo's, Bethnal Green.

Facing page: The North Tyneside Inclusiveness Project was set up in 1997, the cost shared between Barnardo's and local authorities. Here a group with mixed disabilities are pictured on an outing near Gateshead, using specially modified cycles.

Barnardo's Meadows School in Kent received a national Sportsmark award from Sport England, in recognition of its commitment to physical education and sports provision.

Barnardo's 360-plus projects are extremely diverse, tailored to particular local situations and individual children's needs. Like a quilt they are crocheted together – by Barnardo's unique history and experience, its professionalism and dedication, its aims and values. Like a kaleidoscope they reflect each other in loose groups and patterns. Above all they are united by a relentless commitment to excellence. Nobody could have been more concerned about the quality of Barnardo's work than the founder himself: it is another long-established Barnardo's tradition. However, partly as a result of the twentieth century legislation, the nature and criteria of excellence have subtly changed. Though government agencies are now legally responsible for the care of vulnerable children, the law makes little or no attempt to specify the quality of such care. Cash-strapped statutory authorities sometimes provide care that is basic, but little more. Barnardo's would never be willing to provide services that were basic, but little more. This would be unacceptable to Barnardo's ethos and beliefs. So Barnardo's commitment to excellence in the twenty-first century represents its way of ensuring that disadvantaged children do not receive disadvantaged care. Barnardo's believes that such children, of all children, need the most excellent care obtainable. Naturally excellence has its price, and Barnardo's must provide value – to its donors as well as to government authorities. But for Barnardo's, value is based on cost-related quality, not just on low prices and cheapness.

Barnardo's designates the caring work it carries out at each of its sites a 'project'. At some sites, that is at some projects, several different kinds of work may be carried out; other sites, that is other projects, are focused on one particular activity. An example of the former might be the Blackpool Project, which provides parenting skills courses to the parents of young people who have come before the courts, or are in danger of doing so, and also provides outreach and leisure services to disadvantaged children, as well as working with children on an individual basis. An example of the latter would be Meadows School in Kent, which is a residential school for children between 10 and 16 who have emotional or behavioural difficulties and consequently have special educational needs.

As would be expected, many of the projects currently being under-taken by Barnardo's began towards the end of the last century. The sections that make up the Barnardo's quilt can be sub-divided and categorised in any number of ways, but can perhaps best be understood when divided into four principal streams:

- Working with children and young people.
- Working with children in families.

- Working with children in the wider community.
- Campaigning and research.

Here then is a brief précis of the immense range of work Barnardo's now carries out at its 360 or so projects – and you will not find an orphanage mentioned!

Barnardo's work with children and young people

Children and young people have, of course, always been the prime focus of Barnardo's work, and this naturally remains the case today. But today Barnardo's to some extent differentiates between children living in families and children who find themselves alone – usually physically, always emotionally – in a world with which they cannot cope, and which is damaging them.

Homeless children, for example, are usually very much alone. Under present legislation young people have no legal right to permanent housing, and so Barnardo's runs ten projects which offer advice and support for homeless youngsters nationwide. Barnardo's also works with Nightstop, an organisation which runs schemes that offer emergency overnight accommodation for those desperately in need – there are still all too many young 'Carrots' sleeping rough. Having provided emergency accommodation, Nightstop staff then try to find them permanent solutions to their problems.

> *If it wasn't for Barnardo's I'd still be sleeping rough – in doorways and sheds – anywhere I could find.*
>
> Richard, aged 19, now lives in a shared flat.

Barnardo's also helps children who have been subject to sexual abuse – a far from rare occurrence in Britain today. At least 1,000,000 British youngsters are likely to have suffered some form of sexual abuse, and contrary to popular belief fewer than 10% of them were abused by strangers. The fact that most abusers are family members, or family friends, makes it doubly painful, and doubly difficult, for the children to report what has happened to them. Barnardo's runs nearly 20 projects and schemes offering therapy and counselling to help sexually abused children cope with their distressing circumstances.

> *If it wasn't for Barnardo's I wouldn't have realised that I am not a bad person, and that no one has the right to treat me the way my stepfather did.*
>
> Julie was abused from age 2 to 12.

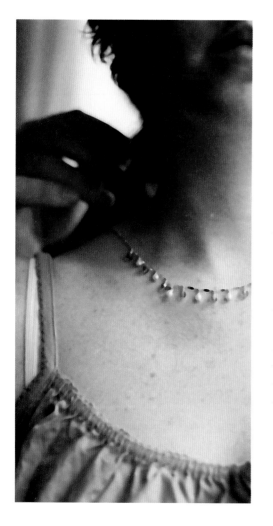

Barnardo's helps children who have been subjected to sexual abuse.

Another form of appallingly widespread abuse is the sexual exploitation of children – children being lured into selling sex. Much of this happens covertly, out of the public gaze – so its prevalence is literally unknown. But Barnardo's experience proves it to be far more common than most of the public realise, among boys as well as girls. The bit the public sees in red-light districts is but a small fraction of the whole. Barnardo's first project to help children abused through prostitution opened in Yorkshire in 1994, and this was swiftly followed by the opening of over a dozen similar projects around the country, as the magnitude of the problem became apparent. Barnardo's projects offer the endangered children a safe, confidential environment where they can escape from their abusers and start to rebuild their lives.

He bought me clothes, expensive jewellery, and told me he'd be with me forever, never leave me or hurt me. But all I got out of it is a drugs problem and lots of beatings.

Jane, aged 16, speaking about her pimp.

Do you think I just woke up and thought 'I'll be a rent boy today'? Thousands of things have happened to get me here – mum leaving, hanging around the pub waiting for dad, blokes trying to touch us up, seeing boys do tricks and getting cash and fags.

14-year-old boy abused through prostitution.

And how many of the public are aware that many youngsters have to care for sick or disabled relatives? Barnardo's estimates there are more than 50,000 child carers in Britain, and 13,000 of them do caring work for more than 50 hours a week. Their average age is 12 – so many are much younger – and most of them undertake their caring role more than willingly, often without realising its effects on themselves. They take on a wide range of work, including shopping, cooking, laundry, paying bills and even providing emotional and physical support – everything from changing dressings to helping their relatives use the lavatory. The intensity of their caring responsibilities can harm their education and social life, strain them physically, and damage them psychologically – minimising their sense of personal identity, and their ability to live their own lives. In 14 centres around the UK Barnardo's workers help young carers recapture their childhood by organising holidays, short breaks and social events, as well as by giving them advice and providing a friendly ear in times of difficulty.

The social services didn't really understand what it's like . . . They just expect mum to get better by herself, they don't really know I'm helping

Thousands of young people spend much of their time caring for elderly members of their family, a devoted activity which can harm their education and social development. In 14 centres Barnardo's workers help them to regain their childhood, tackling a generally unfamiliar social phenomenon.

her. I have to sort out most of the stuff in our house and that takes up most of my time.

Jeet, aged 14.

Much more widely recognised is the extent of youth crime – and how ineffective our society seems to be at controlling it. A staggering 88% of those youngsters who receive custodial sentences re-offend within two years: custody alone manifestly does not stop future criminal activity. Barnardo's runs services which help young offenders make the effort to go straight – this is no soft option for most of them, given their backgrounds – and helps them while they are on bail, a time when they are especially at risk.

Barnardo's also runs services which help young people who have been living in care to adjust to normal, adult life. This can be a very difficult time for youngsters who need to establish new social networks. They need to learn to cope financially, and may have to decide whether or not to repair relationships with their biological families, who they may hardly know. Barnardo's runs 19 services specifically devoted to helping young people of 16-18 who are leaving care, often providing them with accommodation as well as practical help and advice, as they begin to build a bridge from their past to their future.

If it wasn't for Barnardo's I would have no-one to turn to. I would be all alone in the world.

Jackie, aged 18, after leaving local authority care.

Most of the homeless, the sexually abused and exploited, the young carers, the young offenders and children leaving care are helped – have to be helped – on their own. But fortunately a large number of children can be helped while living with families, either their own biological families or adoptive and foster families.

Barnardo's work with children and their families

As it is now accepted that children should stay within their families whenever possible, Barnardo's goes to great lengths to work with the families of children needing help whenever it can.

Ever since Tom Barnardo's time, Barnardo's has been a great helper of disabled and disabled children – and the tradition continues strongly to this day. Few people appreciate the sheer scale of the issue. Despite all the benefits of modern medicine and improved maternity care, over 450,000 children and young people under 19 in Britain suffer disabilities. More than 100,000 of them are severely disabled,

Unlike the problems of young carers, youth crime arouses widespread public concern. Barnardo's runs services devoted to helping young offenders go straight.

with at least two kinds of impairment, and about 17,000 families have more than one disabled child. Disabled children and their families habitually suffer – as they have always suffered – from discrimination, social exclusion and inadequate support. Disabled children's quality of life is deeply damaged by unequal access to education, employment, leisure, housing, and health care. In the twenty-first century, it is a shameful picture.

Barnardo's underlying approach to children's disability can be summed up in a single word: *inclusion*. Inclusion is about access for disabled people in its widest sense – to education and to society as well as to buildings. It is about equality in opportunities and in personal relationships, as well as in facilities and services. Helping disabled children is, as it has always been, very costly. Nonetheless, Barnardo's runs 30 projects which work with disabled children, helping them live with their parents whenever possible, or otherwise in other family units. Barnardo's is the largest voluntary-sector provider in Britain of short breaks – previously called respite care. Short breaks encompass a spectrum of services, from playgroups to temporary fostering, from home-sitting to short-stay residential trips. Short breaks help the children develop social skills and gain experience, while the parents get time out. All this is done by Barnardo's skilled professionals, devoted to working with disabled children. Just as it was for Dr Barnardo, working with disabled children is among the most rewarding of all the work Barnardo's staff does.

Young people from a Barnardo's project in the West Country enjoying sport, 2002.

Domestic abuse is a major
social problem.

We have to live in an integrated world, so why should we be separated?
A lot of people are embarrassed about us, they don't know what to do,
so if we are in a group they can get used to us and be the better for it.

Andy, aged 16, wheelchair user.

Again as in Tom Barnardo's time, the charity today is responsible for
a great deal of fostering, as well as adoptions. Most of the fostering
is now short term, helping children and families through temporary
strains and traumas. But some foster care is long term and permanent,
as of course is adoption. Barnardo's places children from all religious
and cultural backgrounds, but makes particular efforts to help
children from minority ethnic groups, who are often hard to place (as
are disabled children). Barnardo's has over 40 fostering and adoption
projects, covering the country in some depth, and helps thousands of
children and young people in this way every year.

A different kind of work is undertaken by the Families in
Temporary Accommodation project in London. Many homeless
families are housed by local authorities in short-term, and far from
salubrious, private accommodation. Overcrowding is rife. Life is
transitory and uncertain. The children have no privacy, no room to
play, and little freedom. Unsurprisingly, all this can lead to both
depression and aggression. Barnardo's works with hundreds of
families in such temporary accommodation each year, advising them
on how to secure the benefits and grants they are legally entitled to,
sorting out accommodation difficulties, providing furniture and
clothes, and above all helping the children cope with the
overwhelming problems they face.

If it wasn't for Barnardo's we would all still be sharing one room in a
bed and breakfast hotel with no cooking facilities.

Diane, who with her husband Jim and their three
children, has been rehoused with Barnardo's help.

Regrettably the family itself is often the cause of a child's difficulties.
Many children are subject to domestic violence as well as to sexual
abuse. People tend to think domestic violence only affects women.
Not so. In about 50% of cases children are directly or indirectly
harmed too. They may be hurt trying to stop the violence, or even be
the target of violence themselves. In extreme cases domestic violence
can lead to death – the Victoria Climbié case, though especially
horrendous, was far from unique. Violence in the home can continue
undiscovered for many years. Barnardo's provides a range of projects
designed to help abused mothers to look after their children, and
protect them from their partners' violence. The children are taken on

Barnardo's publicises the value of adoptive families.

outings with other kids, taken away for holidays, and looked after at play-schemes. The mothers are given advice and information on housing, finance, and on their legal rights. And in some cases Barnardo's seeks to help the men who behave violently, tackling the source of the abusive behaviour head-on.

Unfortunately, the UK has one of the highest rates of teenage pregnancy in Europe – seven times as high as in the Netherlands. Low education levels, growing up in poverty, and being the child of someone who was herself a teenage mother all increase the likelihood of girls becoming pregnant in their teens. But it is not only poor, under-educated girls who become teenage mothers: it happens across all strata of our society, almost always to the detriment of mother and child alike. Barnardo's now has no fewer than 47 services working with teenage mothers, many of whom are (or should be) still at school, some of whom are homeless, and very few of whom have anything like the parenting and domestic skills necessary to bring up a child properly, let alone several children at once. Nor is it only girls who need to be helped. Young fathers are frequently left out of the equation, but whenever possible Barnardo's supports and encourages them to remain involved with their children, to their mutual benefit.

When I first realised I was pregnant I was in total shock. I didn't know how I was going to cope. That's why coming to Barnardo's was, well, such a lifesaver.

Ruth, aged 15.

Finally, it should not be assumed – and Barnardo's never assumes – that parenting is an easy job which all mothers and fathers can handle instinctively. Far from it. Parenting is one of the hardest jobs there is, and some well-meaning adults simply make a hash of it. Indeed, there are few parents who would not benefit from the help and guidance Barnardo's now provides at 30 different projects throughout the country. These projects run specialist programmes for people from different cultures and religions, organise courses, help those whose children have learning difficulties or special needs – giving parents the skills they need to succeed in doing the job they so want to do, effectively and well. 61% of British parents describe parenting as 'fairly difficult' or 'very difficult'. Barnardo's Family Centres are there to help them.

> *You don't get a rule book to follow, you just give birth and everyone automatically assumes you know it all.*
>
> Christine, who is being helped by a Barnardo's Family Centre.

Young fathers are frequently left out of the equation.

Working with families has become Barnardo's largest area of activity – but there are certain kinds of childcare problem which can only be satisfactorily addressed within the wider community.

Barnardo's work with communities of families and children

Hard though it may be to believe, child poverty in Britain is today three times higher than it was 20 years ago. We have some of the worst child poverty in Europe, as well as the worst child and infant mortality rates. Barnardo's is working to reduce the impact of poverty on children and young people through social, economic and community action. For some communities poverty and lack of opportunity are everyday facts of life. Many large estates have few facilities, while unemployment and crime are painfully high. Children growing up in such circumstances get a lousy deal. Barnardo's runs 40 community development projects, plus eight anti-poverty services which have received National Lottery funding. These Barnardo's centres offer children a safe haven in which to play, and offer their parents a place to meet and talk. They provide day care and play-schemes, after-school clubs and parental guidance. They offer particular help to local disabled children.

Barnardo's is also working in partnership with the Children's Play Council to develop a scheme called Better Play. This is an England-wide scheme with a £10,000,000 grant from the New Opportunities Fund. Launched in April 2002 Better Play aims to deliver the following objectives, for children aged 5-16 years:

- Opportunities for children to play safely in their own localities.
- Opportunities for adults to help in providing children's play.
- Enhancing health and safety in disadvantaged neighbourhoods.
- Sharing and disseminating good practice within communities.

People think if you live in a deprived area you are lazy, or it's your own fault. What they fail to realise is when people are at the bottom of the pile they don't have any self-confidence to improve themselves.

Janet Bonney, Barnardo's Ley Hill Community project.

Barnardo's works in both urban and rural communities, enabling everyone in the locality to be involved in improving their own neighbourhood, and to identify what needs to be done to make things happen, and to make things better. The charity brings pressure to bear to help local communities receive the high-quality services they need and deserve, which leads naturally on to the fourth principal stream of Barnardo's current work: campaigning and research.

Barnardo's campaigning and research work for children

To back up this kaleidoscopic quilt of services, Barnardo's nowadays carries out a great deal of research. Much of it is devoted to evaluating the work done by Barnardo's projects, to make sure they are successful and cost-effective. But the overriding aim of most of this research is to ensure that all Barnardo's work is as *excellent* as it can possibly be. Mention has already been made of the quality of Barnardo's premises and facilities: time and again it has been shown that children react to the quality of their environment. If the environment is broken and dilapidated they will break it down still more and make it still worse. A good environment helps lead to good behaviour.

But of course *excellence* goes far deeper than just buildings and furniture. During the century since Dr Barnardo's death a vast amount has been learned about childcare, and about the best ways to bring up our future generations. Tom Barnardo, though he certainly tried to be as scientific as was possible in his era, was mostly guided by his instincts, and by his religious beliefs. As we have seen, he was astonishingly often right: his native instincts frequently led him to solutions that time and modern knowledge have fully endorsed. But the problems of society in the twenty-first century, and the multifarious difficulties children now face, are infinitely more complex than they were at the end of the nineteenth century, when food, shelter, and training for a good vocation were almost all that poor children could hope for.

Many large estates have few facilities, while unemployment and crime are painfully high.

Today social scientists throughout the world, in universities, in government agencies, and in Third Sector organisations, carry out countless studies into childcare, some of it fairly general, some of it tightly focused on specific issues. As with all research, some of it is first class, some of it less so. Barnardo's Policy and Research Unit studies and sifts all this new data, in order to be able to guide the charity towards the best solutions and towards best practice. And with so many projects of its own Barnardo's is able, through its research, to provide outside practitioners, policy makers, and other service planners with the best available evidence of what works for children, young people and families – and what doesn't. Since 1994 Barnardo's has been publishing a 'What Works' series of reports, which are widely recognised as being particularly authoritative. These reports share Barnardo's experience and other expertise, in order to give all disadvantaged children the best achievable start in life.

Finally, much of this research data finds its way into Barnardo's campaigning activities. Yet again, Tom Barnardo started it. He was fully aware of the need to win public and political support for his philanthropic aims. Similarly the present Barnardo's Campaign Team, like a sophisticated radar system, alerts society to the dangers that threaten our children. Barnardo's Campaign Team has achieved great success in waking up government, and the public, to many of the risks and injustices children now face. Barnardo's 'Just One Click' campaign has greatly heightened public awareness of the burgeoning dangers of

Children need and deserve a happy and safe play environment.

child sexual abuse via the internet and mobile telephone technology; the 'Bitter Legacy' campaign focused on violence to children; 'No Son of Mine' was the first campaign to expose the growing menace of prostitution among young boys, just as the 'Whose Daughter Next?' campaign spotlit prostitution among young girls. These and many other Barnardo's campaigns have generated considerable coverage in the media and often, far more importantly, resulted in positive government action. They bear further witness to Barnardo's total commitment to childcare.

Approaching the centenary of Tom Barnardo's death (though not for that reason) the charity began work on two major strategic, and inter-linked, initiatives which will assuredly launch it into the next 100 years with renewed vigour.

First, participation. Barnardo's has always listened to the children in its care, but it has now begun to give those it serves a much stronger voice than ever before. It is actively seeking the views and opinions of the children, young people, families and carers it aims to help in its activities and decisions. In many ways this reflects the wider trend in society towards consumer choice: whether by way of market research or self-selection, any organisation which aims to serve people well nowadays regularly seeks the views and opinions of those it

Hazel Blears, David Blunkett, and Pam Hibbert, Barnardo's principal policy officer, discuss children in trouble in the UK.

serves. The organisation may not always follow these views and opinions slavishly – it isn't always either possible or desirable to do so. But such views and opinions will be taken into account, and will guide the organisation in its decisions. Why shouldn't the same be true of a major children's charity? Why shouldn't the charity seek the opinions of those it serves – principally the youngsters – and take them into account when making its decisions? Surely this should have happened long ago?

Well, maybe. But for a charity working with more than 100,000 disadvantaged and vulnerable children and young people this is more difficult than it may sound. Which children should be involved in which decision-making processes? What about the very young: at what age should children start to be involved? What about children who suffer educational or behavioural difficulties? How will children respond emotionally to the pressure of being asked to take, or at the very least to influence, important decisions? What legal issues are involved?

Those are some of the difficulties and barriers. Barnardo's is convinced they can be overcome, and is determined to engage children more fully in its work. Children and young people have now started to participate in some of Barnardo's management processes. A UK Advisory Group of Young People called FRAME has been set up,

Cleaning up the community, one of Barnardo's youth community projects.

and FRAME members have attended Barnardo's Council meetings. Finding the best ways of embedding participation deep into Barnardo's operations will take time. But it is unquestionably the right road down which to be travelling.

Second, to help it achieve this aim, and following initial discussions with children and young people, during 2003-2004 Barnardo's drew up what it has called a UK AGENDA. This is an agenda of key issues on which, within its diverse operations, the charity will now concentrate most of its attention, not least because these are issues of clear concern to many of the children themselves. The UK AGENDA has three separate but inter-related strands:

- Mental Health and Emotional Wellbeing.
- Substance Misuse.
- Child Sexual Exploitation.

Barnardo's has of course long been working in all three areas. However it has become increasingly apparent that in the twenty-first century these particular problem areas are growing in magnitude. This is recognised in the new Children Act, and more generally by government, by the social services and by the public at large. Just as

Barnardo's Meadows School
– paintings and pottery.

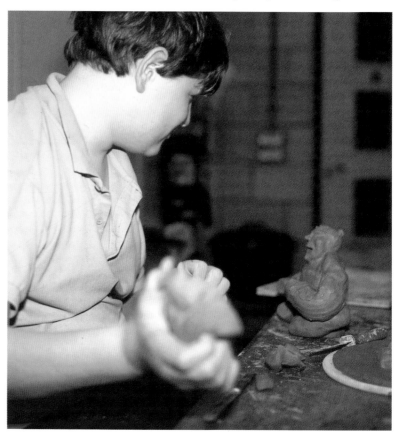

Indoor football at
Barnardo's Meadows School.

child destitution was the major issue in Tom Barnardo's time, the charity's UK AGENDA defines the major issues for children in our own time. Mental illness now afflicts one in four people in Britain, and one in ten teenagers self-harm: this results in 24,000 of them being admitted to hospital each year, and suicide has become the biggest single killer of young men between 18 and 25. The misuse of drugs, alcohol and other substances is proliferating perilously among young people, leading to more mental devastation and sometimes death. Sexual exploitation of children is, as has been shown, in danger of spiralling out of control, and of destroying ever more young lives. There is no magic answer to any of these problems, but the UK AGENDA will focus Barnardo's considerable experience, skills and resources on helping society to tackle them. As a consequence, the UK AGENDA will help the charity increase its understanding and its specific expertise in each area still further.

Naturally all this will cost money – a great deal of money.

Raising the Wind

Remember that Barnardo himself was a wonderful beggar.
Barnardo's Finance Committee Chairman (1957)

While Thomas Barnardo was blessed with an almost super-human abundance of energy and talents of many kinds, it is hardly an exaggeration to say that when it came to fundraising he was a veritable genius. His ability to raise money was prodigious. This was fortunate, because it would again hardly be an exaggeration to say that in his pursuit of the well-being of needy children his ability to spend money was also prodigious. He constantly spent money he did not have, and in later life sometimes spent money when he had been plainly instructed not to do so. As we have seen, when he died in 1905 his charity had accumulated debts totalling £249,000. But against this must be set the £3,000,000 he raised in his lifetime. In 1905 the charity brought in £196,286: the highest level he ever achieved – an extraordinary achievement in just 12 months.

Like other evangelical philanthropists, Barnardo believed the Lord to be the source of all his charitable income. But unlike them, Barnardo liked to help Him in his financial endeavours! This made him unpopular among his brethren. Other philanthropists refused to go out and solicit money, and in his early days Barnardo too insisted that 'We never beg money for the Lord's work.' But this did not stop him encouraging would-be donors by telling them exactly how their cash would help his poor children. From the start every donor of even the smallest sum received a printed and numbered receipt, and all donors were listed in Barnardo's Annual Report – a practice much favoured by many high-powered charities today (except that they generally list only high-powered donors).

In his early years Barnardo struggled hard to keep out of debt. But by the time he published his fourth Annual Report the phrase, 'We never beg money . . .' was omitted. Paradoxically, he fell into debt partly because of the wealthy donors who supported him. To help him house his children they offered him the deeds of

Main picture: A fashion show by Elspeth Gibson raises money for Barnardo's.

Above: Detail of a 1920s photograph.

There is permanent need for volunteers.

Below and facing page: A typical Barnardo's shop.

properties, for nothing. Unwilling to refuse the properties Barnardo then had to find sufficient funds to pay for the care of the children he placed in them. This again is a difficulty many modern charities have faced, in one form or another. Tom Barnardo's own response to the problem was that, since he usually improved the properties, 'The whole matter . . . will adjust itself (*DV*) in a few years.' And in the very long run, he was right. Many properties owned by Barnardo's, purchased long ago, are now of substantial value. Nonetheless, the charity did not escape from Tom Barnardo's millstone of debt until 1916, 11 years after his death.

Initially he did not advertise, or send out begging letters, but as early as 1873 he announced a three-day fundraising sale at the Edinburgh Castle, where people could buy articles made and

contributed by his supporters. This immediately upset his more pious followers. 'We earnestly hope you won't have any raffling', one of them wrote to him. Barnardo characteristically responded by publishing the letter, and replied quoting the Bible, saying he hoped his lady supporters would lay 'their needless ornaments, jewellery and trinkets at the Master's feet.' The sale at the Edinburgh Castle achieved modest success, so the next year he moved the sale to the West End, charged a shilling entrance fee, and in the following years received for sale an astonishing assortment of gifts – from china and curios to clocks and concertinas, from animals and aspidistras to flutes, food and furniture. Thus was born, in a very roundabout way, the Barnardo's chain of retail shops.

During the period of his public battle with Charrington and Reynolds incoming funds began to fall. He then felt he had no option but to chase money more vigorously, albeit to the increasing disapproval of many of his devout supporters. He sought funds at prayer meetings, in sermon after sermon, in article after article, in Annual Report after Annual Report, knowing that his requests worked 'liked water falling upon stone' – that is by constant repetition, as modern advertising agents would put it. Incidentally, once he started advertising, Barnardo was not too kind to his agents, as this letter shows:

Advertising Agents are like the Horse Leach's (sic) daughters. You will recall that he had four and they all cried, 'Give! give!' . . . I think I did very well to send you £150 when you expected £300. I do not think you will get any more money this week . . . I am afraid that until the millennium comes you must not expect to get a cheque on the first of every month . . . we will be a trifle short during the next three or four months!

Barnardo's shops rely on good-quality donated goods.

Barnardo was a pioneer in the use of photography for fundraising purposes. From about 1870 onwards he hired photographers to take the 'before' and 'after' photographs which later landed him in a pickle. Until the Charity Organisation Society's adverse adjudication in 1887 he sold the photographs in packs of 20 for five shillings, or singly for sixpence each. As well as raising money directly from each sale, the photographs carried fundraising copy on their reverse – in effect the purchasers were buying his advertisements from him. In 1874 he opened his own photographic studio, and thereafter used photographs to brighten up his Annual Reports, pamphlets and articles. He also used photographic lantern slides to enliven his talks, and later gave splendid slide shows at his regular meetings at the Royal Albert Hall.

Unable to accept all the numerous speaking invitations he received, he appointed Deputation Secretaries to travel the country and speak in his stead, telling them they must seek out churches with large congregations, where they would be able to raise most money, and instructing them to find free hospitality and accommodation whenever they could. Within a few years he had built up a national network of Deputation Secretaries, mostly clergymen from both non-conformist churches and the Church of England. He provided them with posters and with pew papers to leave on the stalls (all printed in

Young Helpers' League group, c.1900.

Above: A street collection drive, Regent Street, London, in the 1920s.

Below: Independent initiative. Barnardo's Saturday Collectors with an exhibition sandcastle, c.1910.

his Stepney headquarters). Even at the bleakest of times, churches and churchgoers were a generous source of funds.

Barnardo was also masterful at recruiting and motivating teams of collectors. He felt it necessary to collect from rich people and poor people quite differently. To collect from the wealthy he launched his Young Helpers' League. Like everything Barnardo did, the YHL was rigorously organised. The League had rules, badges, banners, a magazine, divisions and sub-divisions, ranks and rewards. Within five years of its launch the YHL was raising £8,000 annually. Encouraged by this success, and knowing the poor gave generously, Barnardo set up street collections to collect from 'the man in the street'. The collectors were all women, and he gave each of them a clearly identifiable box, a notice, an armband, literature and an 'official' authorisation card. He got the police, and uniformed Barnardo's boys, to protect them, as collecting money publicly could be risky. In 1898 he was cock-a-hoop when, so he claimed, the Prince of Wales was successfully 'dunned' by one of his lady collectors.

A few years earlier he had launched Self-Denial Week – another supposedly modern idea. He designed it to appeal particularly to the consciences of his staunchest Christian followers. Families were urged

by Barnardo's publicity, and by clergymen throughout the country, to eat only the plainest food during Self-Denial Week; businessmen were enjoined to travel third class, servants to make small household economies and children to give up sweets and jam – all their savings to go to the charity. Self-Denial Week was soon bringing in £2,000-£4,000 each year. At the same time he was raising money from around the world, particularly from the British colonies, with especially generous financial support coming from Australians and New Zealanders.

In 1899 he introduced house-to-house leafleting followed by a return call, which he swiftly learned was far more fruitful than street collections; and he began leaving collection boxes in people's homes. (The treasured Barnardo's *papier-mâché* cottage collection boxes were not introduced until the 1920s, and are now collectors' items.) He also sent out 100,000 fundraising letters each year – yet another 'modern' approach Barnardo was employing on a massive scale well over a century ago. In 1902, to mark the coronation of Edward VII

Above: Barnardo's shop-front collection box.

Facing page: A selection of the many collection boxes that Barnardo's have employed.

Right: Embroidered bed cover.

Below: Dr Barnardo's Homes booklet.

that year, he invented 'Coronation Waif's Saturday'. Then he dropped the word 'Coronation' and by the time he died Waif's Saturday was bringing in £18,000 a year. After his death the name of Waif's Saturday was changed to Barnardo's Saturday, and by the time of the First World War each annual Barnardo's Saturday brought in over £30,000.

Immediately after Tom Barnardo's death the charity launched a major appeal for £250,000 to wipe out all its debts. But such large appeals were seldom successful. Dr Barnardo himself had always collected the largest part of his money in ha'pennies and pennies, and even, it will be remembered, in farthings. Though the £250,000 appeal failed, the charity began to make money selling Dr Barnardo relics: coins the founder had personally collected were sold, as were shells, sponges, arrowheads, tiger claws and other bizarre memorabilia with which he had personally been associated – even copies of the 1904

Letter of thanks for a donation from a factory to the National Farthing League. The League's Effie Bentham was a devoted and immensely successful fund raiser for Barnardo's for over 50 years. (Note the appreciation she quotes from a soldier stationed in Germany for Barnardo's care of his children.)

DR. BARNARDO'S HOMES.
National Farthing League.
Chief Offices: 18 to 26, STEPNEY CAUSEWAY, LONDON, E.

IT would take 1,000 men, paying one Farthing per week, 125 years to maintain our Ever-Open Doors and Free Lodging Houses for ONE YEAR ONLY.

IT would take 1,000 men, paying one Farthing per week, 266 years to maintain for ONE YEAR ONLY all our Hospitals, Homes for Cripples, Incurables and Convalescents.

National Farthing League poster.

Annual Report, the last he prepared himself, were sold for ninepence each. All these sales brought in a little extra cash – and one cannot help feeling Tom Barnardo would have approved of this final, deathbed fundraising effort.

As with children's services, there were few radical innovations in Barnardo's fundraising operations in the decades following the founder's death – with one notable exception. This exception was the creation of an exceptional woman: Effie Bentham.

Effie Bentham, an ardent Christian from a well-off family in County Durham, first fell under Dr Barnardo's spell in 1892 when she and her two sisters (who had joined the Young Helpers' League) organised a fundraising sale in their home town. The sale was a huge success. Effie was introduced to Barnardo, became an active helper and a trusted friend, and donated a large house in North Ormsby to the charity just before he died, which became a home for 25 girls.

Like Barnardo himself, Effie believed in the potency of dreams. Shortly after his death she had a dream which convinced her that God wished her to raise funds for the charity from the poor, based on donations of a farthing a week. Naturally she knew about the gift of twenty-seven farthings the little girl had given Tom Barnardo in his earliest days. Effie took her idea to William Baker, Barnardo's successor, who promptly asked her to spend a year organising the scheme. It was to be named the National Farthing League. Effie was then in her early 30s, and she worked for Barnardo's running the League for over 50 years.

Effie's dedication and eccentric zeal were reminiscent of Barnardo himself. Her energy was inexhaustible; she pressed everyone she knew

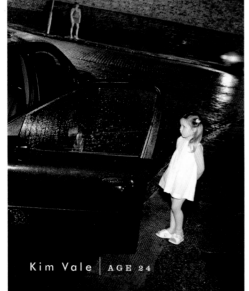

Kim Vale | AGE 24

Martin Ward | AGE 29

Examples of Barnardo's recent challenging
and highly noticed advertising campaigns.
This page: 1999/2000; *facing page:* 2003/2004.

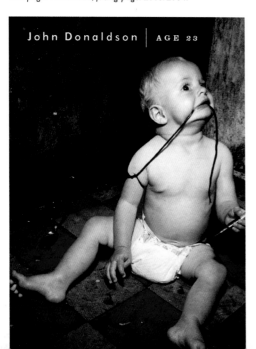

John Donaldson | AGE 23

into her service; she cajoled, exhorted and bullied them into making ever greater efforts; she brooked no interference and supported her work with liberal quotations from the scriptures; she begrudged even the tiniest expense, using old envelopes and even lavatory paper for her official correspondence. And she was unbelievably effective. From the start the National Farthing League's takings grew by leaps and bounds. By the end of the First World War its annual income had reached £33,000, and three years later it soared to £46,000. As the National Farthing League continued to go from strength to strength, in 1925 Effie launched the Sunshine Fund, which was aimed at wealthier people. The Sunshine Fund never took wing. By 1930, despite the economic recession, the Farthing League was bringing in £50,000 a year, while the Sunshine Fund never achieved more than £5,000. In 1939 Farthing League collections had risen to £66,000, and in 1940 the figure hit £89,000 – a staggering feat in wartime. Effie retired in 1956 at the age of 83, and a successor took over and ran the League until 1963. By then the fund had raised over £6,250,000 in farthings, ha'pennies and pennies.

While the National Farthing League was a terrific success, not everything in Barnardo's fundraising garden was entirely rosy. To maximise income Barnardo had encouraged competition between his many fundraising operations. He even printed league tables and charts of results to encourage success and to deter failure – predating the way that salesmen are urged to compete today. But after his death competitiveness frequently got out of hand. Workers in the various fundraising divisions refused to talk to each other, less still to cooperate. Occasionally one division would poach a particularly effective fundraiser from another division. Members of the public were sometimes approached by two different collectors, collecting for competing events, on the same day. Misunderstandings and friction were rife. The county ladies of the Barnardo's Helpers' League (fêtes and garden parties) moved in a different milieu from the fervent, tub-thumping Farthing League collectors (mean streets and factory gate collections). Healthy competition turned into destructive antagonism.

It was not until the Second World War that a Coordination Committee was set up to heal the rifts. In the 1950s collection boxes were standardised, events were synchronised and subsistence allowances were levelled out. As in children's services, professionalism started to come to fundraising. In 1961 a new Appeals Department absorbed the separate divisions, the principals of the divisions retired, and the funds were renamed and revamped.

Almost immediately after the War had ended, in 1946 the Chairman of the All England Lawn Tennis Club had visited Stepney and invited

IF ONLY
EVERY CHILD
IN THE UK WAS
BORN WITH A
SILVER
SPOON

If only poverty didn't crush the spirit and hope and joy of thousands of children every year. If only poverty didn't rob them of the chance of a positive future. If only there was no such thing as poverty. Then there would be no need for Barnardo's to use shocking images. There would be no need for us to ask you to call 0800 032 7222. There would be no need for Barnardo's to exist. If only. www.barnardos.org.uk

Barnardo's
GIVING CHILDREN BACK THEIR FUTURE

Charity Reg. No. 216250

Barnardo's to provide the ball boys at Wimbledon – which quickly became another famous Barnardo's tradition. While the ball boys naturally raised no money for the charity directly, the publicity helped keep up a favourable image of Barnardo's, as the boys were wondrously efficient, disciplined and obviously enjoying themselves. Then in 1959 Barnardo's began selling Christmas cards, and in 1973 – 100 years after Tom Barnardo organised his first big sale at the Edinburgh Castle – the idea of launching a chain of Barnardo's shops was mooted, and was quickly exploited. Initially the shops, like most charity shops, mostly sold second-hand clothes and books. Today the merchandise is far more varied, and the shops sell a fair quantity of good-quality second-hand furniture, as well as electrical and electronic products. Barnardo's now runs more than 320 retail shops, generating sales of over £21 million and making a profit of more than £2 million to help fund the charity's work with children and their families.

Over the years Barnardo's has raised money in almost every way you can think of, and maybe a few you would never have dreamed of: auctions, appeals and advertisements; balls, book matches, bike rides and bequests; fêtes, fashion shows, festivals and flag days; jumble sales and jazz gigs; mailings and mail-order catalogues; raffles and rag days; soccer matches, spelling bees, sponsored treks, star-studded shows, sports days and street collections; coffee mornings, church services, classical concerts, covenants, carol parties and corporate donations; breakfasts, lunches, teas, cocktails and dinners. Barnardo himself invented quite a few of these – and his successors have since done him proud.

Last year Barnardo's fundraising brought more than £70,000,000 into the charity – around 500 times as much as the founder raised in the last year of his life. Much of this fundraising requires expert and experienced know-how, and is carried out by full-time Barnardo's staff – but even more is carried out by Barnardo's great team of 250,000 unpaid volunteer helpers. To every single one of them Barnardo's, and the 100,000 children it directly helps, are inexpressibly grateful. Barnardo's volunteers work selflessly for the charity, and are hugely appreciated. Without their efforts Barnardo's would, quite literally, founder.

(If *you* would like to help Barnardo's to help children, don't hesitate to get in touch. Barnardo's can never have too many grass-roots volunteers – and it is marvellously rewarding work.)

Hand-in-hand with the growth of the Third Sector, over recent years a good deal of knowledge has been accumulated about the nature and mechanics of fundraising. There is even a professional body for

One of Felix Topolski's drawings, used in a Barnardo advertising campaign, April 1970.

fundraisers, the Institute of Fundraising. And there have been a fair number of research studies into charity giving in Britain, which among other things have shown:

- More than 60% of the British population give to a charity in one way or another each year, though this figure has been slowly drifting downward.
- Between them, members of the average British household donate around £90 annually, and this figure has been steadily increasing. Contributions from the households who give to charities have increased by 400% since 1980 – so although fewer households are giving, those that give are giving more.
- Women are notably more generous than men. Just over 70% of women give to charities, compared with just over 60% of men; and on average the women give about £11 per month, the men about £10 per month.
- Though they give less in total, because they have less to give, the poor still give relatively more than the rich. The wealthiest households give under 1% of their household expenditure to charities, the poorest give 3%.
- Nonetheless a small minority of donors contribute the majority of total donations. The 3% of people who give more than £50 a month contribute over half of total donations.
- Those who give most are the upper-middle income groups. 80% of the AB social class each give an average of about £270 a year – over £20 a month. Moreover the rich are twice as likely as others to give time to charity, as well as money.

TV presenter Alex Lovell launches the Foresters Toy and Christmas Appeal in aid of Barnardo's.

Presenter Melinda Messenger launching a fundraising initiative for Barnardo's with Proctor and Gamble.

Fundraiser making a sponsored parachute jump.

Above: Lyness Accountancy practice staff took part in a 120 mile dash to Barnardo's head office in search of six hidden building blocks, representing the key components of a happy childhood, to raise an impressive donation.

Main picture, right: Singer and actress Samantha Mumba took part in the Elspeth Gibson fashion show, with ticket sales going to Barnardo's.

Below: GMTV presenter Penny Smith helped launch a fundraising initiative with Tesco Personal Finance which raised £165,000.

Helping the Homeless – Linda Robson of *Birds of a Feather* launched the Foresters Toy and Christmas Appeal at Bethnal Green Museum of Childhood, 2003

Model Laura Bailey at the Elspeth Gibson fashion show.

The Lord Mayor of London, Alderman Clive (later Sir Clive) Martin, who was a member of Barnardo's council from 1977 to 1996, selected Barnardo's for his charity appeal 1999/2000.

- Though it is widely believed that tax breaks greatly encourage charitable giving in the USA, where tax benefits accrue to the donor, there is little evidence to support the view that tax breaks have the same effect in Britain (where recovered taxes generally go to the charity). However the scope of Gift Aid was greatly widened in April 2000, and this may slowly encourage the British public to give more.

What happens to donors' money? There are nearly 190,000 registered charities in the United Kingdom, and they can be subdivided in a number of ways:

Big v Small: Barnardo's is one of Britain's top ten charities, which between them receive donations worth more than £1,000 million a year, while around 100,000 small charities receive less than £10,000 each. Following the merger of smaller cancer charities, Cancer Research UK is now the single largest charity in Britain, with an income of over £300 million.

Beneficiaries v Activities: just under 50% of all donations go to specific groups of people, like children, the elderly, the blind, the disabled and the homeless. Most of the remaining 50% goes to 'activity'-based charities – medical research, overseas development, rescue services, the arts and others like them.

Specific v Unspecific: some giving is very tightly targeted – anything from a particular crisis or disaster to rebuilding the church steeple; other giving is more broadly based and less specific – the money will go to help cancer research, say, or animals, or the elderly, but the donor will not know exactly how it is used.

Distress v Improvement: the great bulk of charities' cash goes towards people, or sometimes animals, likely to be in distress. However a significant proportion (15%) now goes towards more cerebral causes – the arts, the environment, religious institutions, education and our heritage.

Actor Christopher Parker took part in the Flora London Marathon 2004, raising money for Barnardo's.

Below: Children on the Lord Mayor's Parade.

Angela Lonsdale helping promote 2002 Foresters Toddle for Barnardo's, the charity's biggest mass participation annual event

Criss-crossing the causes and the types of charity is a matrix of different forms of donation which charities like Barnardo's have devised to help them bring in cash. Far and away the most common method of donating to charities in Britain is via street collections, but street collections raise relatively little money (24% of the population gives to street collections, but they account for only 3% of total donated funds). Other popular means of giving which do not raise comparably large revenue are door-to-door collections, and raffle/lottery tickets – though both of these contribute marginally more than street donations. At the opposite end of the scale, only 4% of the population donate by way of covenants, but covenants account for 15% of total funds. Jumble sales and fêtes, payroll giving and even advertising are perhaps surprisingly small contributors: each of them brings in less than 2% of the total, from less than 3% of the population. In contrast, church collections remain strong. They attract in excess of 11% of the population, who contribute to churches in excess of 11% of all charitable funds. And most charities receive sizeable sums of money from legacies.

Tom Barnardo recognised the importance of legacies, almost from the start. While all his ingenious appeals delivered useful cash, within a few years legacies became by far the most profitable source of

In a demonstration of remarkable fitness and courage veterans of the Battle of Arnhem – mostly in their eighties – made a parachute jump near the town to mark the 60th anniversary of the battle, and in doing so raised money for Barnardo's. They are pictured here with Edward Fox who starred in the feature film of the battle.

funds, and have remained so ever since. A bequest form appeared in the 1871 Annual Report, and appeals for legacies have appeared in every Annual Report since. In Dr Barnardo's time legacies were the only individual contributions likely to reach three figures. Today they occasionally reach seven figures. Naturally it usually takes some time – on average seven years – for a bequest once made to reach the charity. This is another key reason why Barnardo's needs, and has always needed, constantly to keep itself in the public eye. Though immediate cash income from advertising is often quite small, long-term income from legacies is often very large.

(Today legacies bring Barnardo's over £21,000,000 annually, approximately 30% of all its donated income. It goes without saying that Barnardo's would be delighted if you, too, were to remember them in your will.)

HRH Princess Anne with Helen Carlton, the manager of the Lawrence Weston Children's Project, and Chair of Barnardo's Council, Dr David Barnardo, 2003.

What Works?

So much effort, so much money, so much caring, so much commitment and so much goodwill go into Barnardo's – but does it all achieve anything worthwhile? A century after Dr Barnardo's death, several hundred thousand children and young people in Britain remain disadvantaged and vulnerable, most of them abysmally poor, many of them abused and harmed daily. Can Barnardo's, or any other children's charity, claim to have achieved any fundamental success when so much unhappiness and suffering remain?

Tom Barnardo was well aware of this sceptical question. This was one of the reasons why, as his boys and girls grew up, he regularly persuaded them to appear in public as living emblems of his achievements. That was why he asked 400 of them to appear at the thirtieth anniversary celebrations in the Royal Albert Hall in 1896, and got many others to appear on the charity's behalf on many other occasions. They were there to convince the public that helping destitute children was not a hopeless task. He himself harboured no doubts:

> If the children of the slums can be removed from their surroundings early enough and can be kept sufficiently long under training, heredity counts for little, environment counts for everything.

But in his heart he must have known things are not always that simple. He knew his disabled children could have their distress alleviated, but they could rarely be cured; from his early experience looking after girls in the large Mossford Lodge home, he knew that just removing children from the slums was not sufficient. He came to realise that for most children life in residential homes was far less beneficial than boarding out, after he had brought up tens of thousands of children in homes. Though he started out with all the confidence and exuberance of youth, he swiftly learned that transforming the abject lives of truly desolate children is exceedingly tough. It was then, and it still is.

The celebrated fashion designer, Bruce Oldfield, is one of several famous ex-Barnardo's children who make an important contribution to the charity.

You hardly need be a qualified child psychotherapist to realise that growing up in Barnardo's care would be loved by some children and hated by others. Some children adore being sent to ordinary boarding schools, others detest it, and many of the complaints made about Barnardo's are not so different from the complaints made by children packed off to spend their formative years in expensive public schools by well-meaning, affluent parents. There are always two sides to this story, as these verbatim quotations from over the years show:

To look at, the (Girls' Village) grounds were lovely – the lawns, the flowerbeds and the almond trees. But there was a high fence and wrought iron gates, and once they clanged behind you, you were shut in and didn't feel free.

Agnes

Until I came to Barnardo's I had been shunted from relation to relation and I finally ended up in the arms of the law. Barnardo's encouraged me to join a band, and for the first time in my life I felt a sense of achievement and comradeship. I played the silver bugle with pride and realised I had finally begun to enjoy life.

Malcolm

This and facing page: Scenes from life in Barnardo's homes in the first half of the 20th century.

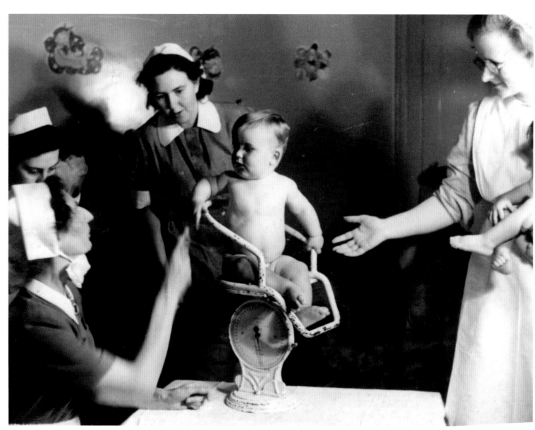

You had no personal life. Everyone was known by numbers. Mine was number nine and everything I had had to be chain stitched with the number nine. What I remember above all was the hardness of the staff. We all had to have pudding basin haircuts and they regularly combed through our hair for lice.

Mary

I came under the charity's care when I was eight years old. I had never attended a school, nor had I mixed with other boys. Men were ogres to me. I was disturbed, distressed and wayward. Under Barnardo's influence all that changed. They taught by quiet example and commitment the merits of self-reliance, integrity of purpose and pride in competency, however lowly the task.

Bill

One of the myths is that the home children were terribly deprived. As children, we had more toys than we could cope with. We had our own swimming pool in the Garden City, our own cinema, films every week, and we usually had plenty of crisps and sweets. I remember one of the kids at school making various attempts to pity me and I retaliated by telling her what we had. She was green. They never

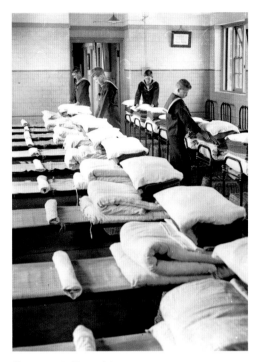

Growing up in Barnardo's care would be loved by some children and hated by others.

punished without good cause, but the punishment was very much as God punishes, the wrath was swift, unexpected, not explained . . . Still I was very attached to the place, it was my kingdom, my domain.

Janet

And the two following quotations, both concerning child emigration, expose the depths of the problem:

If you send out lads and lasses of pluck and principle . . . who from force of circumstances can never rise higher than common servants here, ten to one in the years to come you'll hear such stories of success in life as might put the plot of many a fashionable novel to blush.

Dr Barnardo, 1884.

I hated it. I cried myself to sleep every night. I was cut off from all the friends I ever had . . . I worked like a navvy . . . I got one weekend off in six and the rest I was working . . . I was getting desperate, feeling you're nobody, you're nothing.

Pamela,
sent to the Australian outback and subjected both to domestic drudgery and to attempted rape by the family's eldest son.

Main picture: Best-selling author, Leslie Thomas, pays a visit to his old Barnardo's home in the 1960s. Like Bruce Oldfield and other alumni, he regularly makes public appearances to raise funds.

Inset: Thomas at a Barnardo's children's occasion in 1995.

(These contradictory quotations incidentally highlight both the justification for Barnardo's new-found emphasis on children's participation, and how difficult the process can be.)

An astonishing number of ex-Barnardo's children have written about their life and times in Barnardo's care, and while some of these memoirs are full of bile, many more are deeply appreciative. On this evidence, at least, it seems reasonable to conclude that over the years Barnardo's has succeeded far more often than it has failed. As they grow older lots of Barnardo's children go to considerable lengths to stay in touch with each other, and with the charity, through Barnardo's after-care services. Although the last residential homes closed over 20 years ago, there are today more than 2,000 members of Barnardo's Guild, the Barnardo's alumni club. Many well-attended Barnardo's Guild meetings are held around the country each year. Doubtless, there are hundreds, maybe thousands of other ex-Barnardo's boys and girls who have no wish whatsoever to stay in touch with the charity, or with each other. But this would be equally true of educational establishments of every kind, good and bad. Despite the popularity of old school friends' websites, by no means everyone wishes to stay in contact with their childhood chums. Over 2,000 active Guild members are surely strong evidence that even in years gone by Barnardo's treated most of its children well – in countless cases, very well indeed.

There are some well-known ex-Barnardo's boys who wear their Barnardo's badges with pride. The fashion designer Bruce Oldfield and the author Leslie Thomas, to name but two, regularly make public appeals and raise money for the charity which brought them up. Though author Frank Norman looked back on his nine years in Barnardo's with abhorrence, Leslie Thomas' memoir of his years in care, which is called *This Time Next Week*, is subtitled 'The Autobiography of a Happy Orphan'. Thomas talks of 'the rich vein of family friendship' he found in Barnardo's, as well as 'the inevitable knocks'. Bruce Oldfield, who was taken in by the charity when he was abandoned at birth in 1951, has personally staged several fashion shows for Barnardo's, which between them have raised hundreds of thousands of pounds.

It should never be forgotten that children who found themselves in Barnardo's homes would not have come from the happiest of backgrounds in the first place. Had their young lives been carefree and untroubled they would never have been involved with Barnardo's at all. Reg Trew is an ex-Barnardo's boy, and his autobiography *One of a Baker's Dozen* includes a finely balanced history of his childhood in Barnardo's care. In 1937 his mother died giving birth to her thirteenth child – the Baker's Dozen of the title – and his father was unable to cope. Together with his three younger siblings Reg was taken in by Barnardo's when he was only five years old. Needless to say, the children hardly knew what was happening to them. Reg describes the first weeks torn apart from his father and older brothers and sisters as 'terrifying . . . probably the longest, saddest weeks of my life.' He then remained in Barnardo's care for 13 years, until 1950.

In *One of a Baker's Dozen* Reg Trew writes:

So often when one hears or reads about Barnardo's, there appears to be an underlying terrible sadness to the stories. I suppose this is inevitable, given the circumstances of the 'taking into care' that was at the heart of the charity's work. Our own story has that very sad beginning, there is no doubt, but it is one that produced four well-adjusted, independent adults, eventually enabling them to be reunited in the successful support of a very large family. In short, the 'Trew' Barnardo story is one for which my younger brother, sisters and I are deeply grateful, and in which we think the organisation can take real credit and satisfaction.

Enough said.

David Blunkett, former Secretary of State said in February 2000:

We need to be able to rely on social science to tell us what works and why, and what types of policy initiatives are likely to be most effective. And we want better ways of ensuring that those who want this information can get it easily and quickly.

Anecdotal evidence, of the kind quoted in the paragraphs above, is often descriptively rich and can be deeply moving. But it is insufficiently robust to be the basis for public policy. As former Home Secretary David Blunkett indicated in his February 2000 speech, more authoritative and more reliable data is needed. The report, *Looking After Children: Assessing Outcomes in Child Care*, which had been published a decade earlier, put the point clearly:

A hundred years ago, the benefits of providing separate care for deprived or disadvantaged children were thought to be self-evident. It has since become increasingly apparent that unless outcomes in childcare can be adequately measured, we have no means of justifying the actions of social workers, which may have far reaching and permanent consequences for individuals.

Reg Trew, a former member of the National Council of Old Boys and Girls, wrote about his experiences at Barnardo's, 2003.

The underlying and insuperable difficulty about childcare – about all social work and all the social sciences – is that human beings are infuriatingly wayward and capricious. Unlike the inorganic materials of the physical and engineering sciences, children are unpredictable. Despite Dr Barnardo's confidence in the power of the environment over heredity, the reality is that two children raised in the same environment and in exactly the same way will react utterly differently. The best any social scientist is able to do is to calculate statistically which courses of action are most often, and least often, likely to succeed or to fail. This means that childcare will never be – can never be – 100% predictive and reliable. (We should not wish it otherwise: nobody wants children to be automata.) Nonetheless in the latter part of the twentieth century social scientists have made great strides towards understanding the consequences of remedial childcare, and the long-term effects different courses of action have on children's later lives. Barnardo's has been in the forefront of this vital research work.

In March 1994 Barnardo's, together with the Social Science Research Unit of the University of London, held a ground-breaking seminar called *What Works?: Effective Social Interventions in Child Welfare*. This was effectively a scoping seminar. The papers presented explored the need for much greater measurement of effectiveness in childcare, the problems involved, the extent of extant knowledge, and the attitudes of both social workers and children themselves to research and evaluation.

This seminar laid the foundation for a significant expansion in Barnardo's work in the sphere of childcare evaluation. During the subsequent decade Barnardo's has sponsored and published some 20 influential research studies and papers under the generic series title *What Works?* The titles of some of these Barnardo papers include:

- What works in family placement?
- What works in reducing inequalities in child health?
- What works with young offenders in the community?
- What works in creating stability for looked after children?
- What works in services for families with a disabled child?
- What works? Making connections – linking research and practice.

The *What Works?* reports go a long way towards meeting David Blunkett's call for:

> *. . . social science to tell us what works and why, and what types of policy initiatives are likely to be most effective . . . ensuring that those who want this information can get it easily and quickly.*

Publications in the series have become essential reading for everyone working in childcare, and the series is now widely accepted to be among the most authoritative in the field:

> Barnardo's What Works *series makes a major contribution to the promotion of evidence-based policy and practice. It also has a great deal of value to say to practitioners and managers as they go about making decisions that impact on the lives of children.*
> International Journal of Social Research Methodology

The *What Works?* series comes within the aegis of Barnardo's Policy and Research Unit, which grows in strength from year to year. In addition to guiding Barnardo's own childcare work, and the work of other professionals working in the field, the PRU provides the essential support data for Barnardo's political and social campaigning – such as the 'Just One Click' campaign, the 'Bitter Legacy' campaign, the 'Whose Daughter Next?' and 'No Son of Mine' campaigns, all cited in Chapter Five.

The development of this manifestly valuable area of Barnardo's present-day work will be reinforced by the development of the new UK AGENDA. By focusing much of Barnardo's activity into three broad but relatively specific sectors of childcare, the UK AGENDA will enable the charity to become increasingly knowledgeable in these areas, and to be able to share its knowledge widely. The UK AGENDA will sharpen the kaleidoscopic nature of Barnardo's work. More projects will reflect each other, doing similar types of work in different locations. Comparisons and contrasts will be more straightforward, and analytical conclusions more readily identifiable. This will be boosted by another Barnardo's initiative, which will place increased emphasis on the sharing of learning among Barnardo's quilt of over 360 diverse (but often similar) projects.

Once again an outsider might reasonably wonder why this has not happened before. But even in this digital, internet era the difficulties involved in sharing and comparing knowledge and results, in a nationwide charity, should not be under-estimated. Barnardo's staff are always keen to get on with helping vulnerable children. Sharing knowledge in meetings – or even sitting in front of computer screens – takes up time which could be spent with children. Moreover such activity moves the locus of charity expenditure, however slightly, away from front-line activities to 'management' – not something a wise charity undertakes lightly. All these considerations must be weighed in the balance. As so often, it would be possible to argue that the government, through its various agencies, ought to be doing all this work. And as so often, Barnardo's response is that it may be able to

Abuse of children in the home is as prevalent in affluent areas as it is in poorer ones.

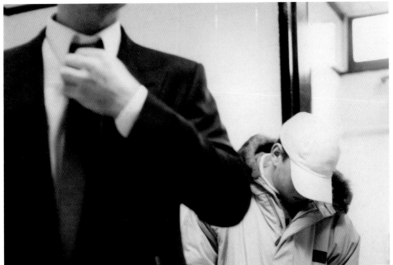

Left and below: Images from Barnardo's press campaigns highlighting the menace of sexual exploitation of children.

do the work better, or at the very least it can supplement the government's efforts to good effect. This was one of Dr Barnardo's principles: don't wait for others, do what needs to be done. It is another tradition still embraced throughout the charity – and it is still right.

Running a charity, like running any other major organisation, calls for endless checks and balances. Barnardo's is stepping up its commitment to evaluating and sharing its knowledge of the effectiveness of different modes of childcare because it is certain this will benefit the present and future children in the revolving door of its care. Of this there can be no doubt.

Passing the Baton

In the century since Tom Barnardo's death, tens of thousands of people – millions of people, if you include all the volunteers – have built upon the founder's great work. So it seems almost invidious to single out a handful of those senior people who have been especially responsible for the charity's long-term success – and they themselves would have been the first to insist that they could have achieved nothing without the magnificent support of their countless colleagues. Nonetheless it would be equally unfair not to identify at least some of those who have found themselves playing key roles in the charity during the last 100 years.

Dr Barnardo's immediate successor was William Baker, who had only just become Chairman of the Council in 1905 when the founder died, though he had been associated with the charity for many years before. Baker was a successful Irish barrister, and was a devout and kindly man. At the end of 1905 he resigned as Council Chairman and took the title Honorary Director, giving up his flourishing legal practice to work full time for the charity without pay. That the charity was in financial difficulties was well known, and it was felt that Baker would, in that time-honoured phrase, be a safe pair of hands. He could be relied upon to avoid running the charity into further money problems. In the event he did better than that, pulling Barnardo's well clear of debt several years before he himself died in 1920.

Some of this financial recovery, however, was achieved at the expense of the physically and mentally disabled children the founder had cared about so deeply. Because they were especially expensive to look after, from 1912 onwards Barnardo's Homes officially excluded mentally disabled children, while the number of other disabled children in care dropped considerably. This the Doctor would have deplored, but it saved money. And in other respects Baker achieved a great deal that was manifestly positive. He sponsored and encouraged the National Farthing League, under the indomitable Effie Bentham. He continued to build and actively develop Barnardo's medical care services. He brought to fruition Tom Barnardo's dream of launching a naval school when

Above: Sally well on her way to a National Vocational Qualification in Food Preparation and Cooking at Dr B's Kitchen.

Main picture: William Baker, who became the Honorary Director of Barnardo's upon Tom's death.

Queen Mary's visit to the Girl's Village Home in 1924. The Hon. Anne Macnaghten greeting the Queen on her arrival. Between them is Miss Beatrice Picton-Turbervill.

Below: Photograph taken on the retirement from the Council of Sir Arthur Smith as Chairman in 1972. Left to right: Douglas Smyth, Director of Child Care; Dr Herbert Ellis, Director General (the one and only person to hold this title which ceased when he left after 15 months in the post); Nicholas Lowe, Appeals Director; Sir Arthur Smith, Theodore Tucker, General Superintendent 1961–64; Vyvyan Cornish, Director of Child Care 1964–71.

he opened Watts in 1906, and added the Russell-Cotes naval school about a dozen years later. He expanded the number of places in residential homes, and opened new homes. Taking over the charity in the wake of Tom Barnardo's death cannot have been easy. William Baker managed the transition with notable skill and charm.

After Baker's death in 1920 however, the management of Barnardo's sailed into choppy waters. The eddies began swirling in the Ilford Girls' Village Home. Two grand and formidable ladies, the Honourable Anne Macnaghten and Miss Beatrice Picton-Turbervill, ex-debutantes both, were appointed by Barnardo's Council to be Joint Governors of the Village Home. Miss Picton-Turbervill was tall and imposing, with a lorgnette, while Miss Macnaghten was dumpy and cheerful. In December 1920 they took up residence in the Girls' Village Home, with their furniture and their maids, Clay and Harris. In the same month Rear Admiral Sir Harry Stileman was appointed to be paid

Director of the charity. The only previous paid Director had been Tom Barnardo himself. Stileman was also a fervent evangelical, and had successfully run Watts for several years. On his appointment as Director he determined that he too would live in the Girls' Village Home. He particularly wanted to live in Dr Barnardo's old residence Mossford Lodge, believing this would underline his status and his position within the charity as the founder's heir. In May 1921 he moved in to the Lodge, by which time the two good ladies were well established and the girls had learned to curtsey as they passed. Almost immediately storms blew up.

The Admiral was keen to make his mark. The ladies were confident and autocratic, and were close friends of many Council members – which Stileman resented. There followed a series of clashes which look quite petty, not to say comic, nearly 100 years later, but consumed the passions of all involved at the time. Mutual antagonisms came to a

A visit to Barkingside in 1972 by Mrs June Ritchie, President of the Women's Auxiliary of Barnardo's in Australia: on the left, Dr Herbert Ellis, Director General, and John Hillyer, right, Chairman of the Executive/Finance Committee.

David Brown, fundraiser, and Pat Perry, Public Affairs Officer, with letters from people who attended the Blenheim Ball, November 1984.

Above: Scottish Headquarters.

Right: Tessa Baring, past Chair of Council, visiting the Ely daycare centre, Cardiff, 1992.

head in November 1922 when, at a special meeting of the charity's Executive Committee, the two ladies read a paper 'practically indicting' the Admiral, and the Admiral replied in kind. Stileman then went so far as to publish a pamphlet critical of the way the Girls' Village Home was being run. This was a step too far. The Chairman of the Council wrote that the Admiral had 'claimed a far more absolute personal authority than Dr Barnardo himself ever claimed' – a statement imbued with a little poetic licence one feels – and in 1923 Stileman left the charity. 'The Director was found generally unacceptable and took his activities elsewhere,' wrote Miss Picton-Turbervill dismissively.

But for Barnardo's, the ladies' triumph had unfortunate repercussions. As a consequence of the Stileman debacle, the charity took fright and did not appoint another paid Director for some 50 years. During that time the Council hugged all key decisions to itself, even though it was composed of part-time, unpaid members. The Council's decisions were enacted through a plethora of committees and a series of General Secretaries and General Superintendents. These downgraded titles were chosen to emphasise that the roles were administrative rather than directorial. Naturally, all this put much strain on the Council itself – there was a period when it met every single Monday afternoon, members taking considerable time off from their offices, businesses and families to deal with Barnardo's problems. (Today the full Council meets some half-a-dozen times a year.) Unquestionably the dedication and industry of Council members over that half-century must have been colossal, as was their workload. But the rather amateurish management structure must also have fettered

Belfast regional office.

Barnardo's development, and constrained its progress during a long period of substantial social upheaval. 'A kindly muddle' was how one staff member described Barnardo's in the early 1960s.

Cometh the hour, cometh the man. Fortunately for Barnardo's, in the 1960s it recruited perhaps its most far-sighted and radical General Superintendent. Vyvyan Cornish joined the charity in 1963 from a background in colonial administration – then the source of many of Barnardo's senior staff. Crisp, clear and kindly, he was determined from the start that Barnardo's could no longer trade on its past glories, and must be dragged – kicking and screaming if needs be – into the new world of childcare that had come about as a result of post-War legislation. Cornish was promoted to General Superintendent a year after joining, and immediately set up a host of working parties to review all Barnardo's activities. In 1965 the Chairman Sir Alfred Owen stated publicly that the mantle of Barnardo's leadership now fell on Mr Cornish, and that Council would support him in every way they could.

It was during Cornish's time in office that many of the transformations mentioned in Chapter Four were effected. The number of children in residence fell steeply, and in 1966 the charity's name was changed from Dr Barnardo's Homes to Dr Barnardo's, while the Working Party on race published its *Racial Integration* report that same year. In April 1968, following another internal report, Barnardo's decided to site its work where it was most needed, moving many of Barnardo's services from London and the Home Counties to the industrial Midlands, the North, Scotland, Wales and Ireland. At the same time Barnardo's old offices in Stepney were shut down and the headquarters moved to the site of the Girls' Village Home near Ilford, where it stands today. In 1970 the decision was taken to start working with mentally disabled children again, after a gap of about 30 years. Then in 1970-71 the Council, guided by the senior staff, resolved to accept non-Christian children without attempting to sway their religious beliefs. All these huge emotional, psychological, structural and symbolic changes occurred in rapid succession under Mr Cornish's leadership.

The internal disquiet which resulted from these whirlwind developments persuaded the Council to appoint outside management consultants. In 1970 the consultants, Messrs McLintock, Mann and Whinney were charged with looking into the structure of Barnardo's, and the relationships between its Council, committees and senior staff. The consultants finally reported in 1971, recommending that a Chief Executive be appointed, with three Directors – of Child Care, Fundraising and Finance – reporting to him. The Council accepted this proposal, and advertised for a Chief Executive. Throughout the

Scenes from a recent day in
Barnardo's Head Office,
Barkingside.

The management committee, 1972: Left to right (standing): Eve Soar, Boardroom Secretary; Keith Manley, Finance Director; F. Graham Harrison; The Rev Desmond Sherlock; The Rev Aubrey Moody; Timothy Lawson, Nicholas Lowe, Appeals Director; Roger Singleton, Deputy Director of Child Care; Mary Joynson, Director of Child Care.

Left to right (seated): Rev Richard Yale; Lady Wagner (now Dame Gillian Wagner), Chair of the Executive Finance Committee; Sir Ian Scott, Chairman of Council; Baroness Faithfull.

country Barnardo's staff were upset at the prospect of an outsider being appointed to run the charity, feeling that the Council was being disloyal to Cornish and fearing that a new boss would herald still further changes. Many of the staff threatened to resign if an outsider was selected. Ironically, as things turned out, Cornish persuaded the staff that it was right for the charity to advertise the new post. He himself applied for the job, and reached the final shortlist of two. The other candidate, Dr Herbert Ellis, was appointed. Ellis was a medical doctor with an excellent record but no relevant previous experience. He was given the title Director General. Cornish swiftly resigned, together with several other senior people. Dr Ellis remained in post for just 15 months, then he too resigned. It was not quite Stileman all over again, as Dr Ellis was personally popular. According to senior staff he simply did not have the know-how to do the job.

The post of Director General was never resuscitated. Instead the Council promoted Mary Joynson, a former Child Care Officer who had

joined the charity in 1970. She was given the newly created title of Senior Director and Director of Child Care, to indicate that she was a first amongst equals – with the Fundraising and Finance Directors reporting to her. Mary Joynson was forthright, determined and able. She proved to be – like William Baker almost a century before – a very safe pair of hands, and provided the charity with a decade of stability and a renewed sense of purpose. She skilfully steered Barnardo's through a politically and financially troublesome decade, before retiring at the end of 1984.

Mary Joynson was perhaps particularly fortunate to be backed in her last seven years by one of Barnardo's most distinguished and capable Council Chairmen, Lady Gillian Wagner OBE, the first woman to occupy the Barnardo's Chair. For a major charity to be headed by two women 30 years ago was noteworthy in itself – though one should perhaps not make too much of this, as in 1979 the country also elected its first female Prime Minister, Margaret Thatcher. Lady

Taken during the Year of the Barnardo Volunteer, 1985/6: David Brown, co-ordinator of the Year of the Barnardo Volunteer; Duke of Devonshire, Patron of the Year of the Barnardo Volunteer and subsequently made Vice-President; Norman Bowie, Chairman of Council.

The houses of the former Girl's Village at the rear of the Barkingside head office.

The Rev David Gamble,
Chair of Council, 1997–2002.

Timothy Lawson, Chair of
Council, 1994–7.

Wagner had joined Barnardo's Council in 1969, in the midst of Vyvyan Cornish's reorganisations, so had experienced the charity at its most turbulent. (In those days it was not unknown for people to remain on the Council for decades, in one case for over half a century. Today Council members are expected to step down after nine years in office.) To become more effective in her work for Barnardo's, Gillian Wagner took a Diploma in Social Administration, having already gained a degree at Geneva University. She was then awarded a PhD for her thesis on 'Dr Barnardo and the Charity Organisation Society', and in 1979 published the most authoritative biography of Tom Barnardo to date (upon which I have leaned heavily, and gratefully, in this book).

In the 20 years since Lady Wagner stepped down, the Chair of the charity has been occupied by five outstandingly able, committed, generous and popular successors – Norman Bowie, Tessa Baring, Timothy Lawson, the Reverend David Gamble and now Dr David Barnardo, a great-great-nephew of the founder. All of them have given generous slices of their time, their energy and their lives to Barnardo's, for no financial reward – believing, with Lord Beveridge, that 'A good society depends not on the state but on its citizens . . . inspired by love of man and love of God.' And all of them have worked closely with the man who has now run Barnardo's for over 20 years: Roger Singleton CBE.

Roger Singleton joined Barnardo's in 1974. He was then Mary Joynson's Deputy Director of Child Care, and on his promotion to the top job inherited a similar title to hers: Senior Director and Director of Children's Services. It is a measure of the complete trust he has earned as Barnardo's leader that he is now called Chief Executive, and nobody is in the least concerned that this grand title might in some way go to his head, causing him to develop Stileman-like aspirations!

During his period working for Mary Joynson as Deputy Director of Child Care, Singleton had personally been responsible for closing many of Barnardo's residential homes, and for absorbing the resulting pain. In the subsequent years he has been responsible, together with his colleagues, for building Barnardo's into its present size and shape. He has led the charity through all of the changes of recent decades which this book has recorded. He has pioneered Barnardo's move into a host of previously unexplored, but absolutely vital new areas of activity. This transformation has been wrought with quiet determination, by evolution rather than revolution. It has been a remarkable achievement, in the fine tradition of Tom Barnardo himself – though except for their shared determination, diligence and wisdom, it would be hard to think of two people with more different personalities than Dr Barnardo and Mr Singleton.

Dr David Barnardo,
Chair of Council, and
Roger Singleton,
Chief Executive, at
the Buckingham Palace
tea party, 2003.

Today the managerial organisation at the top of Barnardo's is almost exactly what the consultants McLintock, Mann and Whinney recommended in 1971 – a Chief Executive, backed by Directors of Child Care, Fundraising and Finance. The titles have been changed slightly, but Roger Singleton and his colleagues Chris Hanvey (Director of Operations), Andrew Nebel (Director of Marketing and Communications) and Ian Theodoreson (Director of Corporate Resources) have proved themselves an exceptionally effective team. Barnardo's has benefited immensely from their contributions, individual and collegiate. Together with the rest of Barnardo's staff and the volunteers, they will launch the charity into its second century since the founder's death – with manifest enthusiasm, justified confidence and steadfast commitment.

A Glimpse of the Future

During 2004 the British government brought forward a significant new piece of legislation which will have an impact on Barnardo's and the care of children for many years to come. Based on the Green Paper Every Child Matters, the new Children Act heralds the most significant changes in childcare for over 30 years.

The seeds of the act were sown following the Victoria Climbié case in 2000, and the subsequent inquiry into her death headed by Lord Laming. Once again it took an unspeakable event to prompt reforms which were long overdue, and which may still not go far enough to achieve their stated aims:

> *To ensure that every child has the chance to fulfil their potential by reducing levels of educational failure, ill health, substance misuse, teenage pregnancy, abuse and neglect, crime and antisocial behaviour among children and young people.*

It will readily be seen that the act's aims overlap with Barnardo's recent UK AGENDA, albeit in different words, particularly in the areas of children's mental and emotional well being, substance misuse and sexual exploitation.

Victoria Climbié was an eight-year-old who died at the hands of the couple entrusted with her care, after many months of torture and neglect. Lord Laming showed that on at least 12 separate occasions during the ten months prior to her death there were opportunities to save Victoria's life which were not taken. Social workers, the police and the NHS failed to cooperate and coordinate their work. Consequently nobody realised the full extent of Victoria's maltreatment, nor recognised the danger she was in. Victoria Climbié's case bore striking similarities to the cases of Maria Colwell, Jasmine Beckford, Lauren Wright and Ainlee Walker, thus establishing that many of the underlying problems were of long standing. The common threads were a failure of the various childcare services to share information, a lack of effective staff training, and an absence of anyone with a

Above: The new Children Act will help to bolster the ability of Barnardo's – and the statutory authorities – to care for vulnerable youngsters.

Main picture: A recent conference.

Drug & Alcohol misuse - plans

- We will work with children already involved in drug and alcohol misuse
- We will work with all children to educate & prevent
- We will work with parents & carers who may be involved in misuse
- We will work preventively with communities

Barnardo's

GIVING CHILDREN BACK THEIR FUTURE

If charities limit the work they are willing to carry out for the state who then will do the vital welfare work that they renounce?

strong sense of responsibility and personal accountability. The new legislation aims to rectify the situation. Its main provisions are:

- The establishment of a Children's Commissioner for England, to be a voice for all children, especially those who are vulnerable. (There are already Children's Commissioners in Scotland, Wales and Northern Ireland.)
- Professionals working with children will be required to co-operate with each other, for the children's benefit.
- An electronic file will be kept on which any concerns about a child's welfare will be recorded.
- Local Safeguarding Children Boards will be set up, on which all relevant local children's services will be represented.
- Every local authority will appoint a Director of Children's Services, and in every local council there will be a lead member responsible for children's services.
- There will be new powers for central government to intervene anywhere children's social services fall below acceptable standards.

In many ways the wheel has turned full circle: several of these provisions are reminiscent of the 1948 and 1963 Children Acts, which failed to operate effectively, despite their well-meaning intentions. Many childcare practitioners are alarmed by the fact that the Children's Commissioner is unlikely to have the power to investigate individual cases without prior Ministerial approval – a government proviso which appears to be either flagrantly self-protective or meanly penny-pinching.

Despite its minor shortcomings, the new Children Act should prove a major step forward in the realm of child protection, and will appreciably bolster the ability of Barnardo's – and the statutory authorities – to care for vulnerable youngsters. Childcare and the social services in the UK have made substantial progress in recent years, and there is every reason to hope this legislation will not falter in the ways its predecessors faltered.

Barnardo's UK AGENDA, and the charity's determination to give children a stronger voice in its future plans, and in their own well-being, will be the main drivers of its activities during the next few years. But the broad, fundamental issues raised in the first chapter of this book have still to be resolved.

Is the magnitude and proportion of state finance changing the role of welfare charities, and if so how? Might the government's proposed expansion of the role of charities, getting them to carry out still more statutory work, be a poisoned chalice? How should charities apportion the funds they receive from the state agencies and the funds they receive from voluntary donations? Perhaps the answer is for charities to limit the work they are willing to carry out for the state, in order to be less beholden to government funds, and to ensure their own independence. Who then will do the vital welfare work they renounce? Have charities any ethical right to turn away social work they know desperately needs to be done, and for which the government is willing to pay them? Are government agencies capable of taking this work back into their own hands, and if they do so will they be able to do it sufficiently well?

Are there perhaps too many children's charities, treading on each other's toes? Surely economies of scale must apply in the Third Sector, as in almost every other part of the economy? In which case should not an attempt be made by the various children's charities to merge, cut overhead costs and deliver better value, both to their donors and to the state? How can this be squared with the widespread belief among donors that when it comes to charities, more size means more waste?

Can the slow decrease in the total number of people in Britain giving to charity be reversed? This might be effected if the UK Treasury were willing to mirror the US tax system, as charity giving there is at least twice as high as it is here. In the United States charitable donations are tax allowable to the donor, rather than to the

Barnardo's is determined to help young people, particularly in deprived areas, to transform their lives.

recipient (as is the case in the UK). For UK donors, copying the US tax system might well increase the attractiveness of giving, and more people might then give. But paradoxically, this might reduce charities' total income, as any increase in donors' giving might be more than offset by the loss of the Gift Aid tax allowances the charities now receive. (The position in the UK is anyway ludicrously complicated, as standard-rate taxpayers cannot personally reclaim tax rebates on charity donations, while higher-rate taxpayers have to reclaim the top slice themselves!) Since donors are, in effect, subsidising government expenditure, surely the situation ought to be simplified? Perhaps the Treasury should allow donors to choose who should get the tax rebates – the charity or themselves?

On a more parochial level: how can Barnardo's shake off its old-fashioned orphanage image, and communicate to the public its kaleidoscopic quilt of services, and the wide-ranging help it now provides directly to over 100,000 children throughout the UK? Having grown so rapidly during the years either side of the millennium, should Barnardo's now put on the brake – or continue to expand as rapidly as it possibly can, to help still more children in need of care? How should Barnardo's divide its funds and resources between front-line childcare, political and social campaigning, and research? How can Barnardo's ensure that it continues to find and employ the very best people, in an economy where hot competition for the brightest and the best means that – despite the attractions of working in the Third Sector – good people can earn larger and larger sums in the private and public sectors with every year that passes?

In whichever ways Barnardo's resolves these fundamental questions, we can be absolutely sure its answers will continue to reflect the determination, spirit and heritage of Thomas John Barnardo – and reflect the charity's present Vision and Purpose:

- To make the lives of all children free from poverty, abuse and discrimination.
- To help the most vulnerable children and young people transform their lives and fulfil their potential.

There is another key difference between the Third Sector and other parts of the economy which sometimes puzzles people when first they become involved with charities. Most organisations seek customers, people with money and a willingness to acquire the goods and services they offer. Charities like Barnardo's do not quite do that. Charities like Barnardo's look for people with no money, people who are sometimes unwilling, at least initially, even to be helped. Just as Dr Barnardo, in his youth, wandered through London's slums at night, attired in his shabbiest clothes and with cake in his pockets, looking for waifs to care for, today – more than a century later – Barnardo's reaches out to children with problems and pain: children whose lives it has proved it can almost always improve.

During the 100 years since Dr Barnardo's death the charity he founded has naturally had its ups and downs, successes and failures: things could not have been otherwise in a dynamic and vigorous organisation operating in a swiftly changing world. Through all its vicissitudes Barnardo's has held true to its founder's fundamental commitment – to help disadvantaged and vulnerable children whoever they are, wherever they are, in the very best ways it knows how. This has not changed. This will not change.

Acknowledgements

There are two extremely good and highly readable books about Barnardo's: *Barnardo* (1979) by Gillian Wagner, and *For The Sake Of The Children* (1987) by June Rose. Both provided me with a great deal of historical information, for which I am immeasurably grateful. I also plundered Barnardo's excellent and extensive library, where Christopher Reeve and his team consistently guided my researches and provided me with generous help, records and data. Kate Gavron provided the initial leads which helped me get going, when I was bewildered about where and how to start. Dr David Barnardo, Roger Singleton, Andrew Nebel, John Tebbet and my wife all read early drafts and made countless improvements and corrections, large and small.

The James & James team made a major contribution in editing, picture research, design and production. Stephen Pover, and Paul Carr provided essential advice and information on images from the Barnardo's archive; they also took the many photographs especially commissioned for the book.

We were very fortunate that Topham generously donated all the scanning of images free of charge as well as supplying their own pictures without reproduction fee.

Finally, I am immensely pleased and flattered that Her Majesty The Queen has provided the foreword to *Keeping the Vision Alive*, and that Barnardo's President Cherie Booth QC has written the introduction.

To have written the book quite quickly, from a standing and pretty ignorant start, demanded a rapid immersion in the history of childcare in Britain over the last 150 or so years, and numerous other people and books unmentioned helped me along the way. To all of them I owe a huge debt of gratitude – but any errors are, of course, my own.

As *Keeping the Vision Alive* was going to press, Southern Asia suffered the Tsunami wave disaster. The swift and hugely generous response of the British people to this horrific event demonstrated once again their instinctive compassion and charity — virtues which have been, and continue to be, of profound benefit to Barnardo's and the children it helps, and to which this book, in its own small way, is testimony.

Winston Fletcher
January 2005

Index

First published in 2005
Copyright © Barnardo's 2005

Published by Barnardo's
Tanner's Lane, Barkingside, Ilford, Essex IG6 1QG
Charity Registration Number 216250

A catalogue record for this book is available from the British Library:
ISBN (Hardback) 1-904659-12-8   (Softback) 1-904659-11-X

Design and Production by James & James (Publishers) Ltd
Gordon House Business Centre, 6 Lissenden Gardens, London NW5 1LX
Project Direction: Hamish MacGibbon
Design Direction: Robin Farrow
Editor: Vimbai Shire
Picture Research: Anna Waddell
Design: Melissa Alaverdy
Index: Ian Craine

Image reproduction by Topham

Typeset in 10.5/14pt Rotis Semi Serif and Gill Sans 8/10pt

Printed and bound by Butler & Tanner Ltd., Frome, Somerset

Photographers
Roy Ainsworth, Piers Allardyce, Paul Carr, Martin Chainey, Marysa Dowling
Robin Farrow, John Kirkham, Ken Lennox, Stephen Pover, Dan Treacy, Jason Wild

Picture acknowledgements
Bridgeman 6, and 8; Getty 3, 4, 5; Guildhall Library 33 (bottom);
Illustrated London News 26; Imperial War Museum 78; Punch 19;
Royal Academy 18; Topham 7, 17, 18, 27, 28, 29, 78, 79, 80, 84.